The Perfect Dog

Raise and train your dog the Mugford Way

DR ROGER MUGFORD

The Perfect Dog

Raise and train your dog the Mugford way

DR ROGER MUGFORD

An Hachette UK Company
www.hachette.co.uk

First published in Great Britain in 2013 by Hamlyn, a division of Octopus Publishing Group Ltd,
Endeavour House, 189 Shaftesbury Avenue, London, WC2H 8JY

www.octopusbooks.co.uk

ISBN-13: 978-0-60062-360-1

A CIP catalogue record for this book is available from the British Library
Printed and bound in China

10 9 8 7 6 5 4 3 2 1

Dr Roger Mugford is widely acknowledged as being
Britain's leading animal psychologist. He holds advanced
degrees in zoology and psychology. After pioneering
the practice of behavioural therapy for pets, Mugford
founded the Animal Behaviour Centre in 1979, which is
currently the biggest of its kind. His methodology has been
embraced by veterinary surgeons throughout the UK.

Roger is a frequent contributor to international symposia,
books, radio and TV programmes about pets. He is
also responsible for the invention of numerous training
accessories, including the world famous HALTI head collar.

Contents

Introduction

This book is a celebration of my 32 years of working with people who have a passion for their dogs, sharing emotions that are as strong as those that exist between lovers or a mother and child. My practice of canine behavioural therapy or problem solving and troubleshooting has given me a privileged insight into the lives and needs of owners wanting to create a better relationship with their dog. We are never so honest and open about ourselves when talking to our doctor, accountant or lawyer as we are when we recount feelings about our dogs, the worries we have and the silly, fun things we do together.

Fortunately, much of dog behaviour is like that of humans, and our anthropomorphic projections onto them provide a reasonably accurate insight into why dogs do what they do. Like children, they have to be educated, stimulated to learn and hopefully to grow into confident, trustworthy adults. The benefit for you is that your pet might get a little closer to fulfilling your ambition of becoming the 'perfect' dog.

The art and science of dog training is rooted in a very simple truism: animals repeat behaviours that have a pleasurable outcome and learn to avoid those with an unpleasant one. I call this principle 'payoffs' and 'penalties', because dogs operate along much the same lines as people, enjoying the payoffs of good food, company or home comforts, as opposed to the penalties of pain, social embarrassment and hunger. Everything we do is governed by the consequences of our actions: drive through a red light and we might die; touch a hot stove and we burn (but we will only do it once!). So it is that a disobedient or troublesome dog learns to do what he does because there were payoffs for doing so – gaining your attention, even if you are scolding him, may be a positive outcome for him – whereas relevant and timely penalties were absent. Dogs are incredibly clever and manipulative when it comes to extracting time, attention and resources from us humans. That is why some owners need help from professionals.

I hope that, after reading this book, most people will know how to change things for the better without going to that trouble and expense. Training and even reforming your dog can really be simple! Broadly speaking, there are two opposing philosophies of dog training today; I characterize them as the abusers versus the amusers. The abusers are those who compel dogs rather than persuade them, relying on the delivery of pain from choke chains, shock collars and the like. But the amusers are just as wrong for their naïve, even sole reliance on reward-based methods and the exclusion of any penalties for dogs that behave badly.

These are extremes: the better approach lies somewhere in between. Sometimes a good parent has to set boundaries to behaviour and assert rules or the child will grow into an unpleasant and unemployable adult. In the same way, over-indulged puppies too often become unruly and even dangerous. Beware of trainers who use an exclusively reward-based approach – they can produce happy dogs but problematic pets. Setting consistent boundaries within which your pet must operate does not mean being cruel or violent; but it is essential for a balanced relationship.

My professional role is to solve everyday behavioural problems that dogs present to their owners. I am very happy to share the technology, the techniques and even the tricks of my trade, with fellow scientists, veterinarians and anyone else with a sincere interest in the welfare of dogs. My greatest hope is that, having read this book, you will understand your dog better than you did, become a more effective trainer and keep him safe in a dangerous world. Consider yourself privileged to have a dog you can call your own…and always consider that he thinks that it is you who belongs to him?

'Animals learn to repeat behaviours that have pleasant outcomes and avoid those with unpleasant ones.'

1 Dogs Past, Present & Future

The truth about dogs

Dogs Past, Present & Future

The origins of dogs – they are not descended from wolves. The evolution of their role in our lives, from worker to companion. The development of breeds. The surprising ways in which dogs resemble us. Dogs' super senses and how we may be able to harness them in the future.

Say 'man's best friend' and we immediately think of dogs. They have earned that title because they are (usually) easily trained, loyal and make useful companions. This book will explore the myriad ways in which the man-dog relationship has evolved and how you can bring out the best in your dog, for his benefit and for yours.

If dogs were really as difficult to live with as their detractors often claim, they would not have become your and my best friend. Living with a dog, your dog, should be an easy relationship that doesn't require great knowledge or training expertise on your part. As I will indicate throughout this book, there is no one right way to create the perfect dog; I want you, the reader, to let your relationship develop as you want it to

Rock carvings such as these from Bronze-Age Sweden show the human-dog relationship dating back tens of thousands of years.

'Living with a dog, your dog, should be an easy relationship that doesn't require great knowledge on your part'

and not in the over-trained and over-disciplined way that you may have been led to believe is 'correct'. This is a book that glories in our dogs' individual personalities and the differences in their relationships with people. It also aims to debunk many of the myths and preconceived ideas that abound in the world of dog training.

My way of training is to be very positive about the benign quirks that your pet develops, but to help to remove the troublesome negative

habits that a few individuals may acquire. I have spent most of my professional life perfecting specialized techniques of behaviour modification and I am going to share them with you. I want you to celebrate your successes and be optimistic about managing those irritating misbehaviours which most dogs (and some people!) have. The key feature of my 'Mugford Method' is that you find a pragmatic balance between *payoffs* that motivate your dog's behaviour and *penalties* that

Myth-Busting: Your Dog Is Not a Wolf

A wolf is often said to lurk inside the brain, if not the body, of a dog, on the assumption that dogs were created by the domestication of wolves, perhaps from several different species and geographical races found in Asia, Europe and the Americas. However, close analysis of their comparative anatomy and especially of their teeth, behaviour and communicatory habits reveals significant differences between dogs and wolves. For instance, the vocal repertoire of the grey wolf, which is found in large parts of the northern hemisphere, is much more extensive than that of modern domestic dogs, but even so dogs tend to be noisier than their wolf counterparts. The territorial bark of 'Who goes there?' has become the nuisance noise of modern dogs, but is rarely heard in wolves. Similarly, the whining of adult dogs seeking food or attention is normal and common, whereas in wolves it is a strictly juvenile characteristic of puppies begging from their mother. On the other hand, the wolf's long-range contact call is unusual in dogs, though they can be trained to perform a wolf-like howl to amuse us or to attract attention.

My experience tells me that if you want to understand dogs, you should study dogs and not wolves. Then why, you may ask, do so many scientists and popular writers preface their work about dogs by comparing them to wolves? The big change in scientific thinking about the dog-wolf relationship came with the recent unravelling of the canine genome and the study of mitochondrial DNA. The latter allows scientists to track relationships between geographically distinct races of dogs, by their breed and the region of the world in which they evolved. That is why we can be certain that at least two thirds of today's dog breeds derive from the Asian protocanis ancestor.

Wolves howl to maintain contact with other members of their pack: one of a number of behaviours they don't share with domestic dogs.

The jaw of a dog (*Canis lupus familiaris*), bottom, and that of a wolf (*Canis lupus*), top, show the prominent canines being distinctive of a wolf.

discourage them. 'Payoffs vs penalties' is the main theme of this book and will provide you with the most certain and effective way to train your dog to do what you want him to do.

How Did Dogs Evolve?

There is a long-founded belief in both scientific and popular literature that dogs are descended from wolves and that your pet is somehow a wolf in domesticated form. I have always been dubious about this theory because the dogs, wolves and wolf hybrids that I have known are all so different: simply put, dogs behave like dogs, not like wolves. I think it is important to question this myth, because it produces an unwarranted fear of dogs as dangerous animals that suddenly turn on their human caretakers, and because it can be used to justify our treating them in a harsh and domineering fashion. What I have found over the years is that a giving and forgiving approach works best for most human-dog relationships.

The Perfect Companion

Keeping a dog as a companion is not some modern indulgence of our affluent societies.

'What I have found is that a giving and forgiving approach works best for most human-dog relationships'

Rather, our relationship with dogs goes back over thousands of years and we evolved together to achieve the near-perfect partnership many of us share today.

Archaeological evidence links dogs to humans in burial sites excavated in Europe and the Middle East from 12–14,000 years ago. However, our recently improved understanding of DNA (which I will talk more about later in this chapter) enables us to estimate that these ancient dogs came in from the proverbial cold and may have hitched themselves to the human wagon even earlier. This seems to have occurred primarily in Asia, where a small but now extinct species *Canis lupus variabilis* provides the missing link between wild and domesticated dogs. Let's refer to this ancestral dog as protocanis, and the key point is that it was not a wolf (see box, page 11).

Dogs give me more pleasure than almost any other facet of my life. Each dog in the 'Mugford pack' found me through rescue or court cases, and are all so different from each other.

The association between early man and protocanis may not have been due to any planned efforts by our ancestors. Rather, they were probably 'adopted' by a small carnivore that benefited from hanging around human settlements. Protocanis could clean up or steal leftover food, gain protection from larger and more dangerous predators and later was in a good position to reap the many benefits that followed the adoption of settled agriculture. In return, from our ancestors' point of view, these early dogs would warn of danger, help in hunts, and even offer hygiene services: by eating human faeces!

So if you wonder why dogs make such perfect companions, are so sensitive to our moods, tolerate human foibles and find fun in almost everything we do, it may be because their association with us goes back much further and more intimately than any other of our domesticated animals. Dogs have, in their special way, become almost as human as humans.

The Diversity of Dogs

Skipping over thousands of years of human and canine evolution, if we now fast-forward to the last 500 years, when there are reliable historical and artistic accounts of dogs with people, we can see that there has been an amazing explosion in the number and diversity of breeds. People have become fascinated with breeding varieties of all manner of domesticated animals: pigeons, sheep, cattle, poultry, goats and, of course, dogs. Clubs were formed of like-minded breeders, and for dogs these became the Kennel Clubs of Great Britain, America and indeed of most countries. Dog breeds quickly became defined by critical physical characteristics, which may have had some bearing on their original purpose to hunt, herd, guard, race and so on, but may no longer be closely connected with these roles.

The pursuit of 'perfection' in the breeding of pedigree dogs has sometimes had unfortunate consequences. A uniform appearance in each

Myth-Busting: Not All Pedigree Dogs Are Unhealthy

Hybrid vigour is a biological phenomenon that is widely exploited in livestock farming, where the offspring of crosses between pure breeds of sheep, cattle and poultry grow faster and are usually healthier than their pure-bred cohorts. Despite a few extremes in the world of dogs, my experience is that most pedigree dogs are healthy and can expect to live to a good age. For instance, we rarely see unhealthy Border Terriers or Jack Russells. However, other breeds such as Golden Retrievers, which are prone to certain cancers, German Shepherds and of course the big-headed English Bulldog are a major challenge to veterinary scientists and to you and to me, who just want our dogs to live a long, healthy life.

Some conditions can be eased by veterinary intervention but only at considerable cost, which is reflected in the elevated premiums charged for insuring some breeds. There are no simple answers to these complex issues, which arise because fashion rather than fitness has guided the selection criteria of judges at dog shows, and 'winning' dogs get to breed more than the 'losers'.

Let's hope that the world's most iconic working dog, the German Shepherd, can be rescued from its decline. Fortunately, healthy, easy-going, companionable German Shepherds do exist, but those who judge and breed poor specimens need calling to account for what they have done.

The characteristics of individual breeds have often been exaggerated in the pursuit of what a few people regard as 'perfection'. The Cavalier King Charles Spaniel's domed skull, the Bulldog's square head and the German Shepherd's nervous temperament are all areas of concern for veterinary surgeons and dog lovers alike.

breed can be created only by the crossing of related individuals, sometimes as close as fathers mating with their own daughters. This inbreeding – which in humans is called incest and is forbidden by law and prevented by cultural taboos – has been tolerated by some dog breeders under the euphemism 'line breeding'. It certainly limits physical variability, but at the price of reducing variation of other beneficial traits. The visible effects often mask

The Role of Genetics

The perils of inbreeding have been voiced repeatedly by geneticists and have come into sharp relief in recent years with media focus upon the most extreme and least fit breeds such as Cavalier King Charles Spaniels, English Bulldogs and German Shepherd Dogs. It may come as a surprise to learn that the German Shepherd is genetically vulnerable, given its massive popularity as a working dog with the police and military. Sadly it probably harbours more genetically determined ailments than almost any other breed, despite experts' best efforts to rid it of hip dysplasia (a painful condition which can lead to arthritis and lameness), spinal malformations, epilepsy and a nervous disposition which predisposes it to becoming an over-protective protector. To their credit, many Kennel Clubs around the world have changed the wording of breed standards so that they encourage better breeding practices and healthier offspring. This might involve the shape of dogs' eyes, the size of a Bulldog's head, angulation of hips and so on. Kennel Clubs and veterinary specialists have a system for registering individuals suffering from hereditary conditions such as hip dysplasia, the eye condition retinal atrophy or epilepsy. Developments in genetic screening enable breeders to be warned of the existence of between 50 and 60 unhealthy genes in the DNA of a prospective sire or dam, before a planned mating takes place. To put this in perspective, there are more than 200 genetic markers of inherited ailments afflicting humans. It seems likely that genetic counselling will become a growth industry as we aim to breed healthier humans and canines.

A comparison between old pictures and modern photographs of the Old English Bull Terrier (top), the Greyhound (centre) and the Labrador (bottom). Many dogs that were originally bred to hunt, guard or herd are no longer much used for those purposes; more recently their characteristics have been selected for form rather than function.

hidden defects to genetic material. Inbreeding favours the accumulation of unhealthy genes which, when they are carried by both parents, often produce life-threatening and disabling anatomical or metabolic defects.

Breed Developments

Most dogs today don't have to perform useful tasks such as ratting, pulling a cart or catching hares. The many different breeds are often no more than a statement of fashion, an expression of beauty in the eyes of their owners. However,

Does the Boxer on the right bear an expression of guilt and remorse, or is he fearful of punishment for his destructive antics?

sensitivity and impulsive temperaments that made them difficult to train. Fashion has changed since the 1970s and now judges favour a smaller, more compact and usually more agreeable animal. There has also been a marked divergence of 'type' between the working and show strains of Labradors, Cocker Spaniels, Border Collies and many other breeds. The working strains can make very demanding pets because of their high energy levels, whereas show versions may present more companionable traits, such as sitting quietly at your feet and sleeping a lot. Working Border Collies are the best example of this phenomenon, as they are programmed to constantly harry and herd livestock, which can be a problem if you don't happen to run sheep on a Welsh mountain!

Dogs in the Modern World

The pace of change in human society is constantly increasing under the dual onslaughts of information technology and urbanization. Overall, dogs have adapted incredibly well to the move from being an ally of prehistoric hunter-gatherers to working as farm dogs, and now to

what was beautiful to European eyes 150–200 years ago may be very different to what we admire today. Old photographs and paintings of dogs show that most breeds have changed massively in appearance over the last hundred years. For instance, look at the Bull Terrier from the 1920s compared to today (see photos, page 15). Of course, there are some breeds

'Dogs have adapted incredibly well to life in small house with exercise in overcrowded city parks'

that have not much changed across the ages. The Greyhound, for instance, has always been subjected to relentless selection for speed over appearance, making it the perfect running machine whose function, rather than fashion, defines its form.

Even in my 30 years of practice as a behaviour consultant, I have seen dog breeds undergo marked changes in both temperament and appearance. When I began my career, show Labradors in the UK were usually heavyweight creatures with over-sized heads, low body

life in small houses with exercise in overcrowded city parks. They travel with us, tolerate obnoxious noises and smells and thrive on weird manmade diets. But what does the future hold for them?

It seems certain that we humans will become an increasingly sedentary species, less willing to walk, run or work outdoors. The historical role of dogs, which was to alert and protect against danger, seems no longer to apply. Instead, we have CCTV cameras, movement detectors and, as the ultimate deterrent, guns. But a dog's secret

Party Trick?

There is a good way of exploring your dog's similarity to us humans: yawning! We all know that yawning is infectious; it is a physiological response designed to increase oxygen supply to the brain and has a strong social psychological component. So it is with dogs, as referenced in a study by researchers at University of London in 2008, who found that dogs tended to yawn in response to their owners yawning.

recipe for coping with this rapidly changing world of humans is to continue with what has worked so well in the past: enhancing our self-esteem, flattering our egos, being funny and just occasionally even being useful.

More Like Us than You Might Think

The rise and rise in the popularity of dogs as pets confirms that today we want them for psychological rather than utilitarian qualities. We seek companionship from the animals in our lives. Dogs can express most of the emotions that

anthropologists consider to be human and those who say, 'He's only a dog' or, in scientific jargon, 'Don't anthropomorphize' may be wrong. My dogs are insanely jealous if we favour one over the other. They are depressed when left, and one of them, PC, even punishes us by being slow to greet us if we have gone travelling without him. Dogs have tempers just as humans do and some wear an expression of remorse or guilt if they have done something 'wrong' or even witnessed another dog in the household breaking the rules.

There are many similarities between how dogs and people react to given situations. Each of us learns from the other and clever dogs soon learn to anticipate our next move, our preferences, the

Humans harness dogs' 'super senses' to hunt everything from criminals to pheasants. A Bloodhound (left) and Cocker Spaniel (centre) trap scent in the muzzle; Greyhounds (right) respond to a mere flicker of movement.

significance of small gestures and changes in our facial expression. Indeed, it is as though those closely integrated, 'special' man-dog relationships can create a canine mind reader. However, there are other sensory issues where it is clear that dogs perceive the world differently from humans.

Special Powers

Dogs have a much greater sensitivity to high-frequency sounds than most people, up to the ultrasonic range of 25 kilohertz and beyond. By contrast, adult humans respond only to sounds up to about 20 kilohertz.

tasks for dogs in blue rather than red. Dogs are exceptionally good at detecting movement, which is useful to a predator for whom the tiniest flick of a rabbit's ears may be the critical cue to direct his hunt for food. But it is in the realm of smell that they really have the edge over us. It matters not whether they are a hundred, thousand or million times more times sensitive than humans; the important thing is that they can focus on particular smells and follow them to source even when they are becoming less intense. That is the secret of tracking by dogs, either homing in on an individual's particular

'The tiniest flick of a rabbit's ears may be the critical cue to direct a predator's hunt for food'

It used to be thought that dogs were colour-blind, although we now know that this is not true. However, their spectral sensitivity is different to ours. At the upper end of the visible spectrum dogs are poor at distinguishing red, whereas they have a good perception of green and blue at lower wavelengths. Their world of colour is rather like human deuteranopia or colour blindness, whose sufferers cannot distinguish red from green or blue unless the objects in question differ in brightness. It would, therefore, make sense to design toys and

smell of sweat, or following the odour of crushed vegetation. Whereas tracking is a practical illustration of a dog's ability to discriminate differences in concentration of chemicals, they can also detect incredibly low concentrations of odorants.

I witnessed this at first hand when I was a post-doctoral researcher at the University of

When two dogs meet, sniffing helps them 'get to know each other', as they pick up important information about sexual state and emotions. Similarly, a dog can learn a lot from the urine-marking of another individual who passed by earlier in the day.

Canine 'Pheromones': Sexy Perfumes for Dogs

There has been great interest in the past few years in the marketing of odours that, allegedly, alter a dog's emotional life. They are often described as canine pheromones, but before we can say that we need to understand what pheromones are. They were originally identified in insects, in which tiny quantities of a certain chemical can dramatically change the behaviour of another insect of the same species. These chemicals are always species-specific and produce predictable responses in the receiving animal. Usually, they are associated with sex, so that a male moth might search for a female who is exuding a 'come and get me' perfume: he will follow it to source, et voilà, sex!

In mammals, behaviour is altogether more complicated than in insects and is affected by learned experiences from previous encounters with particular odours. The smell of urine and vaginal secretions from a bitch in season is attractive to a male dog because he has experienced them before, in an encounter when sex was the happy outcome. Experimental studies have shown that sexually naive dogs (those that have never been mated) are less reactive to the smell of a bitch in season than are sexually experienced dogs. It is wrong to describe the cocktail of chemicals that a bitch in heat produces as a pheromone – rather it is a signal or an invitation to a prospective lover, with the upshot depending on his previous experiences.

Marketeers have exploited the mistaken notion of canine pheromones to modify various aspects of dog behaviour. One product claims to mimic chemicals associated with the mammary glands of a lactating bitch, so that it calms adult dogs in the same way as naturally occurring chemicals might calm puppies suckling from their mother's teats. The experimental evidence of the efficacy of this so-called 'appeasing' pheromone is flimsy, but it is a nice story – would that it were true!

Where such mixtures are effective, they can be explained simply on the basis that the aroma evokes pleasant memories from the past, just as scent evokes powerful memories of past encounters for us, whether it is the perfume worn by a girl on our first date or the smell of our first new car.

After many years of study, I have concluded that complex animals such as dogs, cats and certainly humans are not affected by pheromones in anything like the way that insects are. Nevertheless, certain aromas do influence our emotional and endocrine (hormonal) systems. Aromas from lavender and other herbs may have a demonstrable calming effect upon both people and animals. Dogs love to explore the world using their sense of smell, and have a remarkably good memory for significant odours.

For your dog's greater pleasure I recommend you expose him to many natural and ideally plant-based aromas. Rub the leaves of flowers in your hands and offer them to him to find out those which he likes and dislikes. You will probably discover that his preferences are remarkably like yours: another example of parallel evolution at work in our two species.

Medical Detection Dogs are trained to detect a range of life-threatening medical conditions.

Pennsylvania Monell Chemical Senses Center in Philadelphia. We studied the olfactory skills of a German Shepherd Dog called Max and found that he could detect the presence of -ionone at a concentration of 10-14, which is something like one molecule in a large room of air!

epilepsy or diabetes. The British charity Medical Detection Dogs (MDD) trains dogs to warn diabetes sufferers in advance of a hypoglycaemic crisis. Their work is at an early stage, but they have also trained one dog to warn a lady with Addison's disease of an impending imbalance, while another alerts his owner to life-threatening allergies. The possibilities of dogs being used as a diagnostic aid in human medicine are only now being appreciated by doctors and scientists; it is a new and exciting area of research.

The Curse of Super Senses

Practically speaking, you might imagine that dogs' extreme sensitivity to sound and to smells would handicap them in the noisy and polluted world that we share. Fair and foul noises and smells must, I hypothesize, be the triggers for many behavioural problems. We see this in some dogs exhibiting bang phobias, but quite often city dogs are distressed by more subtle, high-frequency sounds from air-conditioning units, radio emissions, trains, trucks and the

'There are well-recorded cases of dogs and cats travelling hundreds, even thousands of kilometres across cities'

The sense of smell is very important to dogs in the wild, just as it must have been to our paleolithic human ancestors. Nowadays we tend to wash away the natural chemicals that coat our skin and that would otherwise carry information about our individual identity, emotions, sexual state and most importantly about our health. All this data is still available to the more olfactorily attuned dog.

Medical Miracles

It should not surprise us that dogs are able to use their remarkable sense of smell to identify the underlying chemicals associated with cancer,

like. Scented household products can also upset dogs. Individually, any one of these assaults on the canine senses may seem trivial and transient, but in combination and over long periods of exposure they must surely have psychological consequences for sensitive individuals.

Homing Instincts and Lost Dogs

You will have heard about amazing journeys made by animals when they were lost far from home. There are well-recorded cases of dogs and cats travelling hundreds, even thousands of kilometres across cities, highways and natural obstacles. I myself had a cat, Johnny, who

Dogs are equipped with remarkable homing abilities yet are easily distracted in urban environments and can become lost.

Is Your Dog Psychic?

Many people would like to believe that some dogs are so clever and perform such amazing feats that they must possess a psychic sixth sense. Rupert Sheldrake performed interesting experiments to test whether or not dogs are able to anticipate the return of their owners. He concludes that pet dogs perform at better-than-chance levels by becoming excited when their owners are on their way home.

Critics say that there were methodological shortcomings in Sheldrake's tests that, in some inadvertent way, skewed the results or aided the dog in anticipating its owner's return. As far as I am concerned, the jury's out on this issue, because I have seen indications of this behaviour in my own dogs and have had it reported to me by clients. One case that I investigated concerned a German Shepherd who seemed to know when his owner was leaving an office 6km (4 miles) away across London. Was the dog responding to the sound of a rather noisy Volvo driving through town, or to some minute change in the behavioural physiology of the man's wife?

Many of us have seen our dogs wake up in the car as we get close to home or even close to a friend's home that we have previously visited together. This common experience is, I am sure, based on the 'map sense' that I describe in the context of homing pigeons. Dogs pick up on the smells, sounds and then sights of the home environment.

And, of course, as they wake up and give their excited 'you have arrived at your destination' squeaks, we reward them with praise and astonishment at their cleverness.

What amazes me is that some dogs are able to form these homing associations following just one visit to the place in question.

More remarkably still, my little dog PC regularly anticipates my arrival at an address I have never visited before.

This does not mean that he has a 'sixth sense', rather that he is able to detect minute changes in me that signal we are close to our destination. The challenge for me and for science is to identify those signals, be they changes in brain activity, increased sweating or other subtle cues yet to be determined.

Dogs respond to auditory and visual signals as well as picking up on owners' behaviour. Cooking in the kitchen, a car pulling into the driveway and children arriving home, may all be signals that a walk or meal is imminent.

travelled back to a farm we had left six months previously from our new home. Not only was this 30km (20 miles) away, it was separated by a substantial river.

Having found that we were no longer at the old farm, Johnny made the return journey and arrived exhausted two months later at the new address (and thereafter had a pampered and happy life).

The question always arises in cases of this sort: how do they do it?

The subject of homing has been well researched in pigeons, because they are the iconic species that was a vital communication aid in the days before the Internet, even before

However, over long distances pigeons seem to utilize more complex sensory information, which they derive from integrating the sun's position with their own internal clock; they even take account of the earth's magnetic field. Simply put, pigeons carry a biological clock and magnet in their brains, as do dogs and humans. In all probability, Kalahari Bushmen and other nomadic peoples can also navigate by reading the sun and stars, responding to magnetic changes; but when they are closer to home they remember familiar terrain using eyes, ears and nose. The anecdotal and indeed scientific evidence is that dogs use the same hierarchy of senses to find their way home.

'It seems that pigeons, dogs and people have a local map sense, so that we recognize features of our landscape'

the telegraph. It seems that pigeons use the same hierarchy of senses as birds such as swallows, swifts or Arctic terns, which make amazing north-south migrations over thousands of kilometres. Many species of mammals, such as the African wildebeest and the North American caribou, also make long journeys on a seasonal basis, so it is not unreasonable that dogs should be able to do the same.

Pigeons, dogs and people have a local map sense, meaning that we recognize visual features of our familiar landscape and we also glean important ancillary information from sounds and smells. In pigeons, the sense of smell appears to be particularly important and any damage to or interference with it greatly handicaps their ability to find their way home. Experimental studies show that pigeons compensate for complicating factors such as the speed and direction of the wind while navigating their way around many hundreds, even thousands, of square kilometres in their home range.

The reason so many dogs become lost (and are in danger or are picked up as strays) is that they are side-tracked by looking for and finding food, shelter and hospitality from humans. Dogs are socially programmed to seek out the company of people, but if they did not, they would very likely be as capable of long-distance navigation as pigeons.

Future Possibilities

Dogs have accompanied humans on a quite incredible evolutionary and cultural journey, which continues into this ever more complex 21st century. Their emotions are so closely intertwined with our own that they slip easily into our lives and can even come to control us, because they are charming, persistent, but sometimes violent and seemingly impossible to live with. Later chapters in this book will focus on how we can improve the man-dog relationship so that you bring out the best in yours.

2 So you want to live with a dog

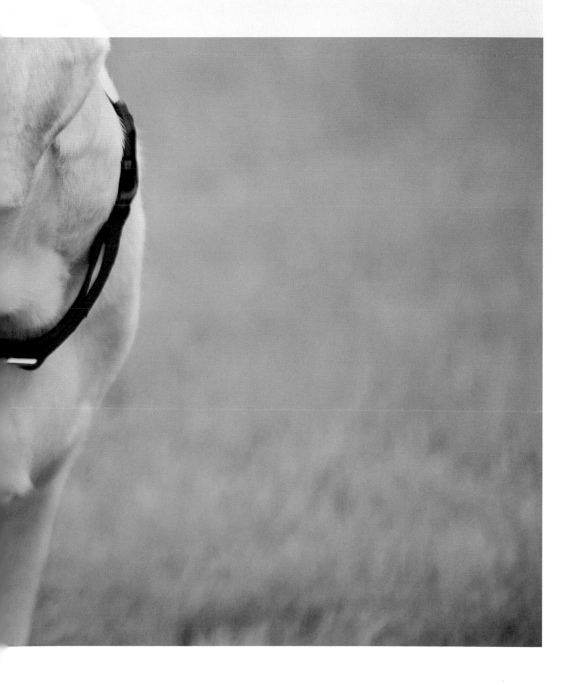

What you should know

So you want to live with a dog

Will a dog fit into your life? If so, which breed? Puppy or adult?
Pedigree or cross-bred? Breeder or private sale? A check list
before you decide. The advantages of adopting a rescue dog.
The importance of socializing a puppy. 'Dangerous' dogs.
Why Breed-Specific Legislation simply doesn't work.

The decision on whether or not to adopt a dog should be one of those life-changing moments that rank alongside marriage, parenthood or home purchase. A dog in your life will have some predictable consequences, though others may be less obvious. You will have less time for other things and something will have to give, be it work, time on the Internet or sports. There may have to be changes in your attitude towards hygiene around the house; dog hair will accumulate in unexpected corners and mud will migrate indoors on his paws.

However, there will also be beneficial changes: a dog provides a new focus of interest for children and their friends, opening the family unit to a wider community and frankly making yours a more interesting household. You will have to spend more time in the healthy outdoors, so you will all be obliged to visit the parks, forests and riversides where your dog would prefer to

'You will have to spend more time in the healthy outdoors, visit parks, forests and riversides with your dog'

Watching your dog and your children grow up together – and spending time together in the open air – is one of the most rewarding experiences I know.

be. There are persuasive medical studies showing that the extra exercise that comes from dog ownership has a positive effect on cardiovascular and other health-related factors. Regular walking at a steady pace for you or a robust pace for the dog will add years to your life. It is also psychologically healing to escape the indoors and commune with nature. A more subtle benefit is that a dog's dust and dander may perk up children's immune systems, making them less prone to allergies and a host of common diseases. Simply put, dogs keep us healthy.

The Best Dog in the World

I am often asked which is the 'best' breed of dog, so I ask in return what is the best type of

Should You Have a Dog?

The following are some pros and cons to consider before you commit to acquiring a dog.

Pros of dog ownership
- Provides reliable friendship and ego-enhancing adoration
- Provides fun: is something to play with and has amusing habits and quirks
- Can be a great social mediator, enabling you to meet other dog owners
- Provides additional security – warning barks act as an alarm against intruders
- Can give practice in 'parenting' for those wanting to start a family
- Can be a sibling substitute for only children
- Multiple working roles

Cons of dog ownership
- Limits freedom, is 'a tie'
- Can be costly in terms of food, vet, grooming and boarding bills
- May damage the home and will certainly mean it is less clean. Dog hair!
- Can raise hygiene issues
- Demands routine, with essential daily chores; long-haired dogs need frequent grooming
- May involve you in legal liabilities if it bites someone or causes an accident
- They die too soon: grief is very painful

car, computer or designer clothes? Unhelpfully, the answer has to be 'It all depends.' Your breed preferences are inevitably conditioned by personal experiences. For instance, I was raised on a farm with working Border Collies, have lived with and loved three gorgeous Irish Setters, but now I have had two decades rescuing and rehabilitating Bull breeds. I adore sight hounds such as Salukis and Lurchers, the latter being a cross between a sight hound, a terrier and a collie. Other favourites are Jack Russells and Border Terriers, and then there are Labradors. We soon learn to love them all!

The wonderful thing about pedigree dogs is that they provide us with tempting alternatives and, like any fashion item, choice of dog is a statement about who you are, who you would like to be and how you want others to see you. There is nothing wrong with this, but it is always worth having someone who is detached and experienced in the world of dogs to guide, play

devil's advocate and point out the pitfalls of this or that breed. The obvious expert to approach is a veterinarian. His or her experience (and in this choose an older vet!) must be worth a fee if you are pointed in the right direction and away from a potentially disastrous mismatch with an unsuitable breed.

Puppies Make Profits

Most people looking to acquire a dog want – or assume that they want – a puppy. But beware. Taking the puppy through its too rapid development is one of the most fascinating experiences you can have and Chapter 4 will look at the optimum strategies for puppy care; for now you need to avoid the pitfalls connected with buying one.

The average life expectancy of a dog is about ten years, which means that in any one year a tenth of the total dog population must be replaced. In the United States that would mean

Pedigree dogs are grouped according to their original function, even though this may no longer be relevant to our pets. The Lurcher and the Saluki (top row) are Sight Hounds, known for their ability to spot their prey at a distance; the Chihuahua and Pug (middle) are Toy breeds – purely companions; the Irish Setter (bottom left) is a Gundog, and some are still used to retrieve game on shoots; and the Border Collie (bottom right) is in the Pastoral group, selected for their herding abilities.

seven million puppies, in the UK perhaps 7–800,000, or in Japan a million. This is a staggering number of puppies and they cannot all come from 'responsible' breeders who go to Kennel Club shows, are knowledgeable about dogs and have a meaningful interest in the improvement of their breed. My experience is that such breeders are generally good people who love their dogs and their breed more than money, and will sell only to people they are confident will provide a suitable environment. Be suspiscious of breeders or kennels that are advertising puppies that are free, or extremely cheap to buy. Equally, be on your guard for very expensive puppies. So-called new breeds of dogs such as the Labradoodle and the Chug have been marketed and are currently being sold the world over but fashion can inflate prices, so beware.

Which Breed?

We live in a media-driven world where Lassie the Hollywood Collie reveals her amazing intuitive intelligence, German Shepherds catch criminals, Border Collies round up sheep and Spaniels find drugs in suitcases. The media coverage of dogs inevitably creates favourites, but spawns prejudice against others, such as Rottweilers and Pit Bulls. The choice of breeds literally runs into hundreds that are registered with Kennel Clubs worldwide and hundreds more that are not officially recognized.

Kennel Club Breed Standards include a short description of the temperament of the breed, but these are usually euphemistic and not always to be believed. There is no single, authoritative source about the typical temperament of a breed; it is a subject of continuing research that throws up different results in different countries. Breed profiles in the United States are probably different from those in Germany, Japan or Australia.

Myth-Busting: Buying on the Internet Could Be Funding a Puppy Farm

Offering puppies for sale via the Internet or a newspaper advertisement is a very easy way to disguise their true source. The seller may offer to do the deal at a 'convenient' location such as a roadside café where you just cannot be expected to make a rational decision – partly because you aren't able to spend time with the puppy before committing yourself and also because you are not seeing it in its natural environment. Or perhaps you will see a single puppy in a home where there are no adult dogs of the same breed. There are many such small-time dealers in puppies whose origins on an unsavoury puppy farm are masked by your seeing them in a false domestic environment.

In the UK, fortunately, scarcely any pet stores sell puppies nowadays, but in, say, New Zealand, Japan, Spain and the US it is normal for puppies to be traded over the counter. These are not the best places to make a puppy purchase! Pet stores do not provide the variety of stimulation and early social experiences that puppies need, which will be discussed in Chapter 4. Instead of going to such sources, I recommend you seek puppies that can have a smooth transition directly from the breeder to you.

Case Study: **Jemma, the Golden Retriever**

Jemma's future owners found her via the internet in 2005. She came with a description of 'gorgeous young puppy from family-oriented stock', and there was a mobile telephone number. Jemma was handed over at a rendezvous just off a motorway, but the problems – and the bills – soon began to mount up.

Jemma had a chronic bacterial infection that required immediate veterinary care. There was also an early indication of a skin disease called demodectic mange and a bad case of worms. Life-saving treatment cost the owners as much as the original purchase price, but worse was to come. By the age of six months, Jemma was wobbly on her hind legs and another trip to the vet confirmed that her hips were a disaster. Hydrotherapy and careful on-leash exercise were prescribed until she was ready for corrective surgery. Jemma had a hip operation at a year old, again at substantial cost.

On top of all this Jemma had never been quite right in her interactions with the family and from an early age was edgy when she was fed and especially in the hour or two after meals. She was referred to me for a behavioural evaluation and advice about her developing aggression. It quickly became apparent that she was hypersensitive to certain ingredients in commercial diets and I advised a home-prepared lamb and rice 'exclusion' diet (see Chapter 7). Jemma's condition improved markedly and we devised a long-term maintenance diet.

Unfortunately, a year later, Jemma raided the garbage bin and ate too many things that she should not have. An instant change came over her and, when a young au pair tried to remove her from the kitchen and the strewn garbage, she attacked. The poor girl, who was alone in the house at the time, was badly bitten and lucky to have escaped with her life. The owners called me for advice, which was immediately to have Jemma euthanized. There could be no question of placing anyone else at risk with such a dog.

Hindsight is a wonderful thing, but it was plainly unwise to have purchased a puppy from a dealer who did not provide an address, a landline telephone or any information about the parents, siblings, and so on. The financial cost of the Jemma experience was astronomic, but that was as nothing compared to the injuries inflicted on the au pair and the emotional trauma experienced by all of the family.

Seeing a puppy interacting with other dogs will help you to make a judgement about its temperament.

Ease of travel has changed the gene pool of dogs as it has of people. Dogs in the UK, for example, used to be isolated from those in the US, Australia or elsewhere, but are now able to interbreed. Pet passports are commonplace and there is a healthy cross-border trade in the semen of pedigree dogs. All these factors reduce inbreeding in what would otherwise be small national populations. Like everything else, dog breeding has gone global.

Just because a dog has ended up in a rescue centre, it doesn't mean he has emotional baggage that will stop him becoming a great family pet.

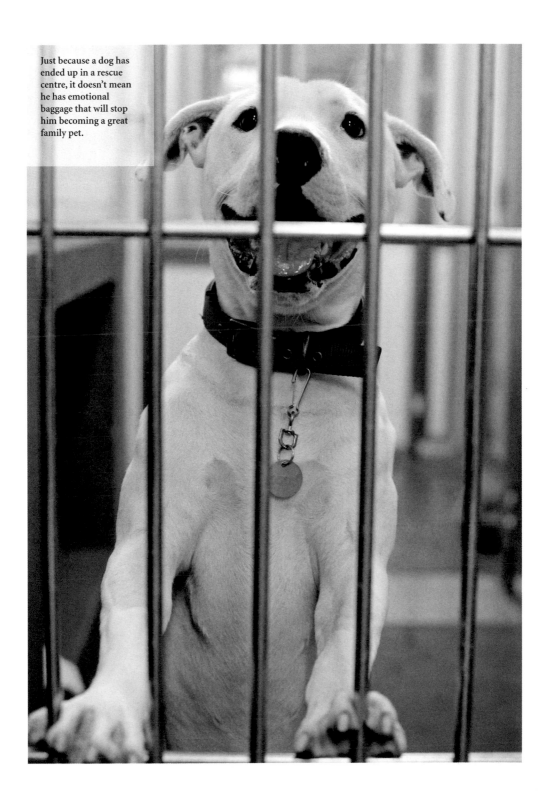

Kennel Clubs keep lists of 'assured breeders' and every breed has its own breed club, which can steer you towards a healthy and well-adjusted puppy, or an adult dog in need of a new home.

Unfortunately, there are many more breeders to whom money does matter, making your needs and lifestyle and the animal's welfare less important than cash. This is what drives too many so-called puppy mills, puppy farms and commercial breeders. They exist in every country and the trade is worth millions.

I once visited a puppy farm in the UK where 5,000 puppies a year were bred from adults living in impoverished kennels, never having access to the outdoors or the freedoms that we know dogs

Puppies and children are made for one another, but only if there is constant adult supervision.

'Stimulation and a variety of experiences at an early age are the prerequisites for a well-adapted adult dog'

need and enjoy. Each of those puppies would sell for an average of £150 at wholesale prices. By the time they had passed through the hands of dealers, Internet sites and the like, they might have a retail value of £500. And whether that figure is in pounds, dollars, euros or anything else, when you multiply it by 5,000 it works out at a lot of money.

The Key Rules of Puppy Purchase

First of all, contact the breeder while the puppies are still young and see them at as early an age as possible. Watch them with the mother and try to see or learn about the father. If possible, contact owners of dogs that were bred from the same parents in earlier litters – they are the likeliest indicator of how this puppy will develop. Be guided by the breeder's observations about the individual characteristics of puppies in the litter. There is no single guide on how best to select a puppy that will turn into the companionable adult dog of your dreams. Despite claims to

the contrary, I have found that so-called puppy temperament tests are poor predictors of adult personality. However, there is a risk that a puppy that will not let you handle him and that retreats from strangers may grow into a withdrawn, fearful or over-sensitive adult. I say 'may' because dogs also have a fantastic capacity for repair and psychological healing. However, the behaviour of puppies gives only a partial insight into how they might behave and react as adults, although there is a lot that an owner can do to make a puppy develop in a positive direction. With an adult dog, it is likely that what you see is what you will get so far as his personality is concerned. So adopting an adult dog is usually a more predictable and less risky strategy than adopting a puppy. And there is a very good alternative to adopting a puppy: it is the rescue dog.

Rescue, Re-homed & Recycled Dogs

All over the world, too many unwanted dogs end up in rescue kennels, more so in some countries

Are Amateur Breeders Bad?

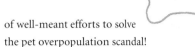

So, having outlined the payoffs and potential pitfalls of sourcing a pure-bred puppy, what are the other options?

The curious paradox about the modern commercialization of the trade in puppies is that in former times many people bought them from neighbours or family who had accidentally or intentionally mated their pet bitch with a local Romeo who was also likely to be someone's well-loved pet. Both sets of dog parents would usually have possessed family-orientated personality traits that would have been passed on to their progeny. So it was that family pets were bred from dogs who had been selected for their companionable qualities, rather than for their looks (or for money).

Highly successful spay-neuter campaigns in most developed countries have nearly closed off this traditional source of puppies for would-be pet owners. The rationale is to reduce the number of surplus puppies that end up in rehoming centres or being killed. However, professional breeders and puppy farms have filled the commercial void left by the passing of amateur breeders: an unintended consequence of well-meant efforts to solve the pet overpopulation scandal!

However, even today accidents do happen as bitches in season go in search of willing males for sex. There are also those who intentionally cross-breed: the most popular crossings of recent years have been Labradors with Poodles (to produce Labradoodles), but there are also Spaniels with Poodles (Cockapoos), Pugs and Chihuahuas (Chugs) and so on. Genetically speaking, these F1 hybrids can develop into highly desirable adults, but it should not be assumed that all such crosses or even mongrels are totally free of the numerous inherited diseases that can affect dogs.

The optimum environment for the raising of puppies is a home where there are children, cats, other dogs and lots of activity. Stimulation and a variety of experiences at an early age are the prerequisites for a well-adapted adult dog. So if you are buying a puppy via this route, favour the pet home where you can see the whole litter and be certain that the people involved are not undercover agents for a commercial dog-breeding enterprise.

than in others. Because of a cultural bias against neutering dogs, there are enormous surpluses in Ireland, parts of Eastern Europe, Greece, Spain and indeed throughout the Mediterranean region. The USA also produces too many dogs for the homes that are available, whereas in Canada it is more likely that a dog will remain in his home for life and not be dumped or killed.

Very few surplus dogs are found in Switzerland, the Netherlands, Germany or Scandinavia, these being countries with high standards of animal welfare or which regulate pet ownership by enforcing licensing and animal-control laws. While every country has national charities running dog-rescue operations, there are also many small, inspired local centres that deserve support. Even if you don't end up adopting a dog from such a centre, you can at least help them with money, donations of food or volunteering time to walk dogs waiting to be adopted. Spread the word and 'do your bit' to empty these rescue centres of dogs and give them a better life as companions in a loving home.

I visit a lot of rescue centres in all parts of the world and am constantly overwhelmed with sadness at the number of lovely dogs gazing out, yapping incessantly to grab a moment of my attention that just might bring commitment and a new home. I have to remind myself that we already have four 'rescue' dogs, and is that not enough? But such occasions always remind me of the tragic issues involved. In Spain there are too many Galgos dumped by would-be hunters. In the UK, there are overwhelming numbers of Bull breeds and especially Staffordshire Bull Terriers that are unlikely ever to find homes: too many Staffies have to be killed each year in British dog rescue centres. Ex-racing Greyhounds are also super-abundant in dog rescue homes the world over. Situations like this should make all of us think once, twice and more before allowing any of our dogs to breed.

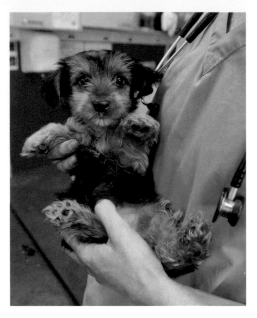

Ask the staff at the rescue home, or the dog's foster carer, or vet if there is one to tell you as much as they can about his previous history and breeding.

Questions to Ask, Tests to Make

Unfortunately, dogs cannot provide us with an honest account of their previous lives and owners, but kennel staff in rescue centres can gain useful insights into a dog's past and may have information left by the previous owner. Before committing yourself, take your prospective dog for a walk or to an enclosed paddock and see how he is with other dogs. Give the usual commands to 'sit, stay and give me a paw'. Does he respond or ignore? Ideally

Myth-Busting: A Rescue Dog Is Not Necessarily a 'Problem' Dog

It is often assumed that if a dog has ended up in a re-homing sanctuary, it must have emotional baggage, be prone to behavioural problems or be a veterinary liability. This is not generally my experience; most of the rescue dogs I see have no more nor fewer behavioural issues than dogs that were adopted as puppies.

A dog may come to a 'rescue' home not just because it was a stray or was rejected by a feckless previous owner. Its owner may have died, been ill, unemployed or overwhelmed by changed circumstances. Each breed has its own rescue organization and if you are set on adopting, say, a Pharaoh Hound or a Rottweiler, contact the national or local breed club and there will be a representative who knows where a suitable dog can be found near you. The movement of dogs between states in the USA, or from Ireland to England, is becoming increasingly commonplace, where charities have found there is a demand for dogs that have been temperament-tested, vaccinated, neutered and generally checked out. We own such a dog, Bounce, a goofy, wonderful Labrador brought from the West of Ireland to England by the charity Dogs Trust.

Case Study: **Dexter, the Cretan God Dog**

I am a big supporter of the educational and animal rescue work performed by the Greek Animal Welfare Fund (GAWF). On one occasion GAWF sent me to Crete to review conditions in a chaotically administered 'rescue' centre, where 80–100 dogs were kept together. There had been many bloody dog fights, some deaths and distressing conditions from which virtually no dogs were being adopted by the locals.

Those who died were mainly the young, old or sick, killed by the stronger dogs in the group. Dexter was one of the more dominant ones, having evolved an extraordinary range of social skills and leadership qualities that seemingly made him immune to the constant conflict and enabled him to rise above the goings-on of the other dogs in this hell hole.

Dexter had become a clear favourite with the staff who did their best to care for this colony. I chose him to appear with me on a TV show where I was demonstrating dog training, care and safe control. He performed marvellously and became a minor local TV star. I couldn't leave him behind when my project in Crete was completed, so GAWF and I arranged for him to be flown to northern Europe, along with the other dogs who were all dispersed to good homes in France, Switzerland, the Netherlands and the UK. After six months in British quarantine, Dexter took up life on my farm as though this had always been his calling.

He never once chased a sheep, fouled indoors or stole food. However, the dominant side of his personality was evident in the way he dealt with my other dogs and my family. He would not tolerate being pestered or challenged by another dog, though he achieved control with a steely look, only rarely by actual fighting.

He also did not like to be restrained for grooming or even held to fix an injured paw. He had learned to bite and he meant it! So I set boundaries to regulate what he could and could not do. He had to sit and wait while I fed my other dogs, and grow accustomed to being held on a lead, having his teeth examined and lying on designated beds but not mine. I persisted and within weeks he transformed into a dog who could be trusted with my young twin sons, accepted that he did not need to win 'skirmishes' with every new dog and knew that there were ample resources of food, shelter and love so long as he adhered to key rules.

Dexter lived with us for a happy 11 years and was a perfect example of a dog's remarkable survival skills in the face of adversity. There are thousands of dogs who experience similar deprivations, yet thrive when transplanted into a normal domestic routine.

get a canine professional to make a more formal evaluation by exploring the dog's response to food, a bone, being lifted, having his muzzle held or teeth checked. Most important is testing the unknown dog's response to other dogs, cats and livestock, all potentially hazardous activities unless conducted by a competent trainer with access to specially trained 'stooge' animals.

But how can you be certain that a dog is safe with young children? This can only be determined from the dog's known history, followed by a cautious introduction to children with the dog muzzled. In a kennel environment it is also difficult to assess whether or not a dog is house-trained or what his response to separation from people will be. Some re-homing

Dogs at professionally run rehoming centres should be evaluated by skilled trainers and behaviourists but it will always be difficult to predict how they will react in a home setting.

Social Skills Have to be Learned

Just as children learn their life skills through play with other children and with adults, so do puppies. The process is termed socialization, which would have happened naturally when dogs were free to roam and to interact with dogs, other animals and with people. The advent of cars and the practical need to keep dogs safe on the road has denied them the opportunity to learn about life as dogs used to do, so we have to compensate by devising new ways to educate social skills in our puppies.

In less developed and rural countries, dogs are relatively free to roam and to meet other dogs and people in their village. I have seen this myself in Bali, where dogs have wonderfully developed social skills and are rarely violent towards people, chickens or the many other animals they meet.

The key to having a confident, friendly adult dog is to invest in puppy training and social introductions at as young an age as is practicable. So as soon as your vet indicates that your puppy has sufficient immunity to the key canine pathogens, take him for walks to the park, trips on trains, meet all manner of people and of course meet lots of other dogs.

Less formal puppy socialisation classes are nowadays laid on by many vets and dog schools. with the serious objective of promoting trusting attitudes to all the kinds of people that there are. Good playschools are not just about play.... instructors will also teach you how to train, restrain and calm your puppy when required.

However puppy training cannot rely only upon formal schooling, but rather has to be woven into all of his early experiences at home and indeed everywhere. It can't begin early enough because investment in your puppy's social skills education is more important than any amount of obedience or trick training you may try to impart later on in his life.

Getting to know other dogs is a key part of your puppy's socialization training. Introduce him to as many as you can.

Dogs should react calmly to being confined to a crate: as long as they have a blanket and a favourite toy, they will be comfortable and can keep themselves entertained. It should be a safe place they choose to go to and not a place of punishment.

organizations explore this issue by placing a dog in a small furnished room and watching his reactions on closed-circuit TV. Unfortunately, this may give only a hint to his response: he may feel very differently about being left alone after a few days or weeks in a new home, when he has become attached to his adoptive family.

A useful insight into broader aspects of a dog's temperament can be gained by watching his response to confinement, be it in a crate or being tethered. There are times and places when a dog has to be tethered: most learn to tolerate this, but others panic and chew through the lead in order to escape. Test him and see what he does.

More information about a prospective adoptee's behaviour can be gathered if he has been kept in a foster home, rather than being institutionalized in a kennel. Many rescue organizations recruit a network of fosterers, who get to know their canine charges and want them to be matched with a suitable pet parent. That person could be you!

And what if he fails? As the case of Dexter illustrates and as I will show in later chapters, there are many opportunities for resolving training and behavioural problems; it is not

'rocket science'. On the other hand, if in doubt about his safety around children or other animals, it is better to say no and look elsewhere.

One, Two or More?

A singleton dog may make many more psychological demands on you than a pair. Dogs are social animals that cannot be set aside when you leave for work, go out in the evening or just want to live a life. Their situation therefore changes for the better when they find friendship and fun with a second or third canine companion. But know when to stop, because too many dogs in the house may spoil your quality of life, deny you normal freedoms; and will certainly keep you poor.

On the other hand, a single dog will probably form a closer, more dependent relationship with you. And when it comes to training, it is much easier to deal with a singleton. Never buy a pair of litter-mate puppies, who will find more fun in one another than with you. Purchasing puppies should not be like a proverbial two-for-one supermarket discount offer.

Breedism

People become fond, sometimes overly fond, of their particular breed and assume that if one Setter, Schnauzer or Bull Dog works well then two must be even better. Not so: the evidence is that dissimilar dogs are more compatible with one another than two or more of the same breed. Little and large, young and old or opposite sexes seem to work best.

You might imagine that in an unequal contest it would always be the larger or stronger dog that 'wins' in the dominance stakes. Again, not so, because social dominance in dogs is not determined just by size or strength. In play we often find that is it the larger dog who handicaps himself so that his smaller playmate can sometimes 'win' chase-tag games, object-possession or tug of war. Having a variety of sizes, sexes, temperaments and ages gives us many more interesting insights into canine behaviour than having dogs of the same breed.

Sibling rivalry or in-pack rivalry is a horrible situation for dog owners. Fights between dogs in the same household are often the most bloody. Conflict is much more likely between evenly matched dogs and is worst between same-sex siblings. Go for opposites!

Dogs, Taxes and the Law

The media often emphasizes the dangerousness of dogs in society; maybe a child was mauled or neighbours are afraid to walk the streets. In reality, deaths and serious injury from dogs are a rarity compared to accidents and mortalities from other causes. Whereas at most two people per year are killed in the United Kingdom by dogs, many more are killed or injured by horses or even cattle. Everyone understands that horses are powerful, unpredictable creatures that often kick, bite and buck to cause life-changing injuries and, in too many cases, even death. And yet, we don't have legislation for the better control of 'dangerous horses' or even dangerous cats, whose bites are usually more serious to humans than dog bites. The teeth and mouths of cats carry a high bacterial burden that reliably introduces

---

Factors to Consider: a Check List

Before committing yourself to taking an individual dog home, it is only fair to you and to him to have satisfactory answers to the following questions:

- Size: is he right for you and right for your home?
- Strength: does he walk on the lead nicely or pull?
- Personality: is he naturally friendly or fearful of strangers?
- How does he respond to children? Introduce him carefully, perhaps with a muzzle.
- What are his social skills with other dogs like?
- Age and health: can you afford the vet bills?

- How is he likely to react to your other pets? Will the family cat leave home?
- Does he know about simple obedience? Does he respond to 'Come' and 'Sit'?
- Does he tolerate grooming and close handling?
- What about tethering and confinement?
- Transport: is he well behaved in the car?
- Food: does he guard?
- Bones: test his reactions with help from a canine professional.
- What is his previous history? Ask kennel staff or foster carers for anything they know.

Opposites make good housemates. If you want more than one dog, go for different breeds, different sizes and different sexes.

infection to people, though bites from a dog are more likely to be disfiguring.

Dogs are the only domesticated animal species to be saddled with controlling legislation. Most countries require owners to purchase a dog licence, which is a sort of tax that others do not have to pay. My view is that the money collected from dog licences should mostly be re-invested into providing facilities for dogs and their owners, or at least into education about pet care, training and help for agencies who tackle the surplus dog problem by discouraging breeding and assisting adoption of unwanted dogs. Education rather than legislation is the way to create a better world for dogs in society.

Breed-Specific Legislation

The concept of Breed-Specific Legislation or BSL started in the United States, where it was (wrongly) believed that certain breeds posed a greater danger to people than others. Bans on Pit Bulls were introduced on a city-by-city or sometimes state-by-state basis. The idea then spread to other countries.

The Dutch Experience

In the 1990s the Netherlands introduced legislation that focused on banning fighting breeds, in particular the American Pit Bull Terrier. Yet it did not apply to the related or visually similar breed of American Staffordshire nor to the smaller Staffordshire Bull Terrier, which has always been popular in the Netherlands.

The Dutch government recruited an army of 'experts' to supervise the legislation and to decide which dogs were or were not Pit Bull Terriers. Many hundreds of dogs were seized and kept in state-financed kennels. If an owner objected to their dog being euthanized, it had to be kept in kennels for the remainder of its natural life and at public expense. Fortunately, the irrational and unpopular legislation was eventually questioned by academics with an interest in the epidemiology of dog bites, and was repealed in 2008.

Immediately afterwards, I was contacted by a well-known Dutch behaviourist who was concerned that so many dogs that had (in his words) 'gone crazy while living out their lives in kennels' would be returned to their owners to live freely in society, with no particular controls. In fact, his fears were not realized and there is currently no need nor appetite for breed-focused controls on Dutch dog owners. However, there is in the Netherlands a very strong interest in dog training and in responsible, welfare-oriented dog ownership. It is that recourse to education and persuasion that is seen as being the best way forwards.

The Italian Experience

In 2003, Italy placed specific controls on a staggering 92 breeds of dog (none of them of Italian origin!), including the 'usual suspects' of Pit Bulls, Rottweilers and German Shepherds, along with Border Collies and even the diminutive Corgi of British Royal Family fame. The list was later narrowed to just 17 breeds, but after finding that there was no reduction in dog bites or associated problems, the government repealed the legislation in 2009. However, new legislation has sensibly placed civil and criminal responsibility on dog owners for any damage caused by their dog.

as 'status dogs'. Several other breeds, notably the Staffordshire Bull Terrier and their various mixes, have been confused with Pit Bulls and the legislation has pulled in any number of mongrels that have been condemned to die on the basis of their appearance, despite being responsibly owned and having a good temperament.

You need to know that I am a fan of all Bull breeds and that Humphrey, my Staffie cross, for all his wickedness, is an adorable companion and a great dog to have in the family. Our civilized society accepts that the temperament of people is not determined by racial or physical characteristics (not even red hair!) and nor is it in dogs. The British legislation is so bizarre and so cruel in its application that I was convinced that, within a year or two of its introduction, it would be repealed. Instead, more than 20 years on, Parliament and our unfortunate police are

'Our civilized society accepts that the temperament of people is not determined by physical characteristics'

In the words of Under-Secretary for Health Francesca Martini, the Italian conclusion was that 'the measures adopted in the previous laws had no scientific foundation. Dangerous breeds do not exist. With this law we have overcome the black list, which was just a big fig leaf (over the larger problem) and we have increased the level of guarantees for citizens.'

The British Experience

The UK Dangerous Dogs Act of 1991 bans the owning, trading or breeding of four breeds: Pit Bull Terriers, Japanese Tosas, Dogos Argentinos and Filas Brasileiros. This legislation has been an utter disaster because it has actually increased the attractiveness of owning a 'banned' type of dog. Pit Bulls were made more desirable by being described in the media and by the police

setting aside more and more resources to pursue the daft objective of ridding the nation of a type of dog that was intended for fighting. And the number of reported dog bites is higher than ever.

The British experience should be a warning for other countries to steer well away from BSL. Nevertheless, breed-specific bans exist in Ireland, France, some parts of Germany, Denmark, Australia, Ontario Canada (about to be repealed) and some American cities (Denver being an example). All are encountering the same problems as have beset BSL elsewhere: it just does not work!

Dangerous Dogs: Those that Bite

The situation regarding genuinely dangerous dogs does everywhere need to be addressed, if only because it is an expression of antisocial

Clockwise from top left, a Doberman, a Pit Bull, an American Staffordshire and a Rottweiler, all breeds that are widely regarded as 'dangerous'. However, in my view the commonsense approach to 'dangerous' dogs is to 'punish the deed, not the breed'. Owners of dogs that have bitten should certainly take the consequences, but it is ridiculous and cruel to assume that every Rottweiler and every Staffordshire Terrier is a threat to other dogs and to people. Incidents involving violent behaviour need to be assessed individually.

behaviour that can set neighbours against one another and divide communities. My view is that owners of dogs that have bitten and injured someone should be liable for the consequences of their pets' behaviour, just as parents should be accountable for the actions of their young children. Of course, the question arises as to whether the sanction should be directed at the owner or the dog, and I favour the former!

If common sense were to prevail, courts would require an objective and informed analysis of how a particular incident arose and whether any of the humans involved might have prevented it. Was somebody bitten because they intervened in a dog fight? If yes, one could argue that the victim should have known better than to put his hands between a pair of fighting dogs. Was the dog encouraged to bite and was it used as a weapon? That is criminal conduct that should be dealt with as an assault with a weapon (the dog). Many prosecutions arise because an owner has tethered his dog in the street, perhaps to go shopping. That can be a mistake, because dogs feel vulnerable and deserted when tethered alone, and their behaviour becomes unpredictable. These are all issues where courts have to rely upon the expert evidence of someone who understands why dogs do what they do. This must not be biased in favour of one or other party to a dispute.

I often have to provide such evidence in court after analysing scenarios similar to those described here. I generally find that sympathetic justice is meted out to dogs because judges and magistrates are usually fair-minded people. But there have been some horrible exceptions. There was a time in medieval Europe and later in colonial America when courts tried animals for various crimes and often sentenced them to death. I find it strange that in this allegedly enlightened 21st century we are still putting animals on trial, rather than dealing with dog-related incidents as straightforward challenges of training and behaviour.

The most obvious alternative to killing a dog is to punish the owner and require that a dog that is considered dangerous wears a muzzle in public places, perhaps until he has had focused behaviour modification from a canine professional. This might be either with its original owner or with a new owner if the dog has been confiscated by order of a court. If we abandoned BSL and adopted these measures, we could spare owners a great deal of worry, improve police-community relations and save a pile of taxpayers' money. Yes, of course, serious incidents involving dogs do sometimes happen, but rarely is it dogs that are at fault.

The behaviour of any dog that bites or is likely to attack needs to be dealt with, whatever breed it happens to be.

3 The Man-Dog Relationship

Pay-offs and penalties to guide behaviour

The Man-Dog Relationship

Your dog wants to please you, but may also be keen on having his own way. The concepts of dominance and hierarchy. The basics of training: payoffs and penalties. Gentle commands, aversive stimuli and how to stop him pulling on the lead! The good and bad sides of technology in training.

Dogs have evolved over the centuries to integrate themselves into family life. They are happiest when they are a loved and loving member of your 'pack'.

'Just as the family is the basic social unit for humans, so the pack is for dogs'

Dogs are one of the most successful domesticated species on the planet. They have shared our ups and downs, our comings and goings over many thousands of years and will continue to do so as evolution exerts its extraordinarily creative effect by acting on the individual who reproduces the largest number of viable offspring. Your dog is the result of competition to reproduce, which has equipped him with talents and tendencies that suit him to life with us humans.

The most significant factor here is that we share similar social organizations. Just as the family is the basic social unit for humans, so the pack is for dogs. As owners, we insert ourselves into the complicated set of rules that govern our dogs' social dynamics, while they cunningly insert themselves into our family lives. Fortunately, the majority of dogs are more keen to please us than are most human family members. Dogs also have a well-developed sense of fair play, of justice versus injustice. If you fail to acknowledge and reward a behaviour which in the past has met with your approval, they will be disappointed and have, in a sense, been unjustly punished. And then there are the inevitable mistakes and accidents: you have trodden on his paw or trapped his tail in the door. What should you do? Of course you should give lots of sympathy, sincerely apologize and confirm to the confused dog that you are a just and kind person.

There are countless anecdotes, some of them true, of dogs showing selfless behaviour in defence of people. Shared loyalties quickly turn into an emotional commitment to the dog that is comparable to and may even exceed the love we show to members of our family. Too often, I have

social relationships between dogs and their people. Unfortunately, some extremists whom I have nicknamed the 'Treat Taliban' pretend that social hierarchies in dogs don't exist and that the notion of dominance-subordination in dog behaviour should be discarded. Nothing could be further from the truth! I myself delivered a paper at a conference held in honour of the late Nobel Laureate Konrad Lorenz in Vienna in 1999. Lorenz's excellent books are peppered with anecdotal observations of the many dogs with which he lived. Whereas descriptions of dominance are given a very full treatment, love or dependency between our two species gets barely a mention. This is all the more surprising to me because it was Lorenz who coined the term

'There are countless anecdotes, some of them true, of dogs showing selfless behaviour in defence of people'

heard clients say that they love their dog more than their spouse or a parent and that their grief after the loss of a dog was worse than they had experienced on the death of a parent. The man-dog relationship is made of powerful stuff.

'Good Dog versus Bad Dog'

This is a daft distinction! A dog that barks, bites or chases sheep is not a 'bad' dog; rather it has simply discovered that certain resources and benefits follow from engaging in these behaviours. Dogs are opportunists and our role as owners is to steer them towards situations where the payoffs from engaging in desirable behaviours exceed the penalties of unwanted behaviours. It's all about payoffs and penalties!

Dog Hierarchies Do Exist…!

In recent years we have seen the rise and rise of reward-based training, which is often more about learning tricks than about establishing satisfying

imprinting to describe the powerful attachment of young birds and mammals to their parents. He gave the iconic example of a clutch of goslings so imprinted upon him that they followed him into a lake. However, I do not count myself among those who deny that social hierarchies exist, and for the avant-garde 'treat and train' dog trainers this may be an inconvenient truth.

Left to themselves, two or more dogs will sort out a pecking order. Acknowledge the hierarchy in the group.

Exposing the belly may be a sign of submission – but also a good excuse for your dog to have his tummy tickled!

Close contact with his owner, praise and a rub behind the ears are all payoffs for good behaviour.

… But They Needn't Lead to Aggression

Watch dogs in the park and see how one will pick up a toy or stick, then willingly give it up, without a struggle, in response to just a gaze from another, more dominant dog. Object possession and repossession is the easiest way in which to monitor social hierarchies in dogs. The scientists Scott and Fuller in the 1950s used a bone-repossession test as a means of

been women who ruled in the home and men who were in charge in the workplace. But even 60 years ago, and certainly today, there were and are myriad complexities about who does what, when, why. So it is with dogs.

If you have two or more dogs, you should acknowledge these social hierarchies and play along with them, not try to interfere or undermine the social status and psychological needs of the alpha dog. If you consistently favour

'If you consistently favour or support the less dominant dog, you will probably create social instability'

defining hierarchies in the several breeds they studied in Bar Harbor, Maine. One bone, two dogs and clearly one will succeed over the other. However, such a one-size-fits-all approach can be misleading, because there is more to social dominance in dogs than mere object possession. In family life, we humans vary our deference or leadership roles depending on the time, place and context of our meetings. In the world that existed before women's liberation, it may have

or support the less dominant dog, you will probably create social instability, which means dog fights (see Chapter 6).

Making the Hierarchy Work for You

Good dog owners work with and within the rules of social dominance, not against them. However, that does not justify the use of physical force, pain or any form of violence against the dog. Actual fighting within a stable group of dogs

Myth-Busting: Dominance – Useful Construct or Misleading Metaphor?

If you read an old-style book about dog training, you will find liberal use of the word dominance, and the need for us humans to be the 'leaders of the pack' being presented as the single most important factor governing the man-dog relationship. According to this view, it is a wimpy owner who fails to gain respect from a dog that runs away, won't get off the bed, bites the hand that feeds it or barks uncontrollably in the car. A popular TV programme about dogs shows a trainer taking on so-called dominant animals by grasping and roughing them, putting them into a subordinate 'roll-over' posture and even helicoptering them on a choke chain until they pass out. In one particularly revealing episode, the trainer is seen to 'take on' a Golden Retriever that defended its food bowl. The trainer earned himself a nasty bite to the hand because he needlessly provoked the now frightened dog, rather than pursue a more gentle, less confrontational strategy. This is all scary stuff, always counter-productive and inconsistent with the way in which dogs are programmed to get along with people.

Whereas the notion of social dominance in dogs may have been over-emphasized by writers and dog trainers in the past, other more interesting aspects of the human-dog bond have been neglected. One such dimension is attachment theory, first developed by the child psychiatrist John Bowlby in his studies of mother-infant bonding in people. We all hope that our dog will become attached to us and reciprocate the attention and time we invest in him. We are flattered at his signs of sadness as we leave home and at his joy when we return. If there is no such show of affection, then we can reasonably ask what is the point of having a dog that seems not to care about us?

Critics of the dog-owning culture have sometimes suggested that we anthropomorphize the emotional capabilities of dogs and consequently give them a status they do not deserve. That view does not, in my opinion, apply to most of us dog lovers, though of course there are the eccentric few who do take their passion to excess. We have all seen reports of marriage ceremonies for dogs, specialist canine gourmet restaurants, insanely expensive dog hotels, bejewelled collars and so on. Yet I would argue that, in moderation, indulging your dog is no more worthy of criticism than showing kindness, consideration and measured generosity to family or friends.

Well-intentioned interventions by owners and having a dog on a lead can predispose dogs to fighting.

It isn't always the larger dog who wins a tug-of-war: sometimes he will yield the prize to his smaller friend.

My dogs may defend their home range – our garden – against visitors. I have a Pet Corrector in case they do.

should be a rarity and most disputes are resolved by a look, a growl, a deferential turning of the body or an appeasing, teasing play-bow. And yet so many of the tenets of dog training were built upon the notion that owners or trainers had to inflict pain using choke chains, electric-shock collars and other such instruments.

Early trainers such as Konrad Most spawned a horrific catalogue of torture methods to 'compel' dogs to do this or that: 'training' was equated with 'avoiding pain'. In reality, dogs are too clever for such a 'brawn over brains' approach, and the mantra should be never to hurt the dog, ever! The obvious reason is that you depend for your long-term relationship on his trust in the gentleness and rewarding outcomes of a touch by your hands, the tone of your voice and the benefits of sharing a secure relationship. Hitting a dog with a stick, hand or foot can only destroy that trust, and with it the prospect of achieving long-term beneficial goals. When it comes to dog training, you need to have a range of pre-planned strategies designed to produce positive outcomes. That is the purpose of this book, and of this chapter in particular.

Payoffs and Penalties

Consider your own behaviour: what makes you tick, what makes you get up in the morning, go to work or perform chores around the house? There are payoffs, maybe money, perhaps feeding your ego, making someone in the family happy, putting food on the table or playing games. These are just some of the positive outcomes that motivate human behaviour.

But there are also penalties. It may be that there are sanctions if you don't go to work. I once worked for a large corporation that paid a 'good time-keeping bonus' to employees who arrived on time. In reality, it was a sanction, the punishment of losing ten per cent of salary for those who were late. Was the 'good time-keeping bonus' a payoff or a penalty? It depends on your point of view, but the outcome was the same. Everyone drove at insane speeds in order to get to work on time!

Parents understand very well the motivating power of material possessions, privilege or money, if children are to perform key tasks. You could call this bribery, but don't expect your child to clean his bedroom, polish shoes or complete homework just from a sense of duty. Dogs are much like children in this respect, and we have to devise worthwhile payoffs that will produce desirable outcomes. The good trainer and dog owner also has to become skilled at spotting what motivates his dog, which must be an individual matter. Here are some examples of payoffs that are important to a dog.

are more motivating than a large amount of a less enjoyable food. Most dogs prefer moist to dry food, and liver is usually the overall tastiest ingredient, so a moist liver treat must be the most motivating of all. But there are massive individual differences in taste: American dogs seem to like peanut butter, while others will go for chicken liver and garlic or maybe

'American dogs seem to like peanut butter, while others will go for chicken liver and garlic'

Treats

Food is usually the number-one motivator and fortunately it is a reward system that can be timed and metered according to the dog's response. Most of us feed dogs a main meal once or twice a day with extras allocated for treat training, but if you wanted to you could give him all his daily food allowance as a reward during training, with little or none left for meals. The choice is yours.

The size of a treat is not the only consideration when trying to influence your dog's behaviour; it is its taste or palatability that makes the difference. Tiny quantities of great-tasting treats

just a carrot. Test your dog for his likes and dislikes and – within reason – let him decide! Some brands of dog treats are designed to provide a defined amount of energy, so that you can calorie-count and avoid overfeeding. A 10-kg, middle-aged terrier requires approximately 700 calories per day, about a third of the healthy energy intake of a small person. This provides you with an opportunity to give your dog many rewards in one day. In the training regimes described later in the book, you will see that the 'little and often' approach is my recommendation for early-stage training; hence my preference for micro-treats.

Research your dog's likes and dislikes. Keep high-value treats to reward important behaviours.

The payoff: Charli is given a treat for paying attention during training. Occasional use of treats helps to build a positive relationship.

Play

The British veterinarian Mike Fox coined the expression 'If you play together you will stay together.' He was right and of course dogs love games. It is for you to find the activity that excites your dog. The extraordinary scent-detection skills of dogs on the lookout for drugs or explosives are usually driven by the prospect of just a few minutes' play with a squeaky toy or tennis ball. Detection dogs are usually Springer Spaniels, whose sole motive in life seems to be to chase and retrieve objects. No self-respecting Bull Terrier or Mastiff would 'work' for such a trivial reward: they would rather destroy the tennis ball, then wait for something better to come along!

Whether the chosen game is throwing and retrieving a toy or a few minutes' rough-housing or tug-of-war, it should always be you who manages it, both initiating and ending a play session.

Social Recognition

Sigmund Freud coined the terms ego, id and superego, referring to the sometimes contradictory nature of human emotions. Dogs are not really much different; ego certainly plays a big part in canine motivation and it is the ego that craves recognition, praise and admiration from others. Dogs often live in an uncertain world, but just a look, touch or a gentle word from you can lighten their lives and bring joy. The simplicity and honesty of the canine character are perhaps their most endearing traits.

But this desire for attention means that when we intervene to stop unwanted behaviours such as stealing a treasured object or chasing birds, we are in fact rewarding the very behaviour of which we disapprove: our attention has been caught, which may be exactly what the dog wants. The term for this conundrum is Inadvertent Reinforcement of Unwanted Behaviour, a good example of the Law of Unexpected Consequences about canine behaviour. It is the key to understanding why dogs do what they do, especially when it is not what we want them to do. It is also why a reprimand or even physical punishment is so often counter-productive.

Withdrawal of attention is one of the most powerful ways to punish a dog. Psychologists usually refer to this as 'time out', where a child or dog is left alone. Alternatively the mother or dog owner may turn sharply away and avoid contact. There is no need to give a smack or shout a reprimand; just the withdrawal of company, eye contact, voice or touch is sufficient punishment.

Comfort

Dogs love their creature comforts, whether it be a warm spot in winter or a cool one in summer. Then there are beds, ideally your bed, which are plainly much more desirable than sleeping on the floor. Access to such comforts can, with skill and patience, be a payoff for behaviours of which

Dogs love to sit on their owner's lap or beside them on the sofa. It's important to make them realize that this is a privilege rather than a right. Pay-offs (left) and penalties such as ignoring (right) should be linked to appropriate versus inappropriate undesired behaviour.

you approve. Never let coming onto your bed or beside you on the sofa be taken for granted. At the very least, make your dog 'sit' and 'wait', then only 'come' by invitation. Devise your own word and hand signals, perhaps a tap of the sofa for 'on', then pointing to the floor for 'off'. You are in control, but you make your dog happy by allowing him these privileges at a time and a place of your choosing.

run free in Japanese parks or countryside, but I have seen the efforts which responsible Japanese dog owners make to go to private places or clubs where their pets are free to socialize with other dogs.

The quality of walks is as important as the duration or distance. Let your dog sniff the paths taken by other dogs, watch and dream about chasing squirrels, find but hopefully not kill

'Let your dog sniff the paths taken by other dogs, watch and dream about chasing squirrels …'

Activity

The freedom to roam, run, explore and do all the other things that dogs love to do is something we have to allow. The rattle of a lead, picking up keys or putting on walking clothes and boots become obvious cues for dogs to take to the hills, forests and parks. For most dogs, this will be the highlight of their day and it is an absolute responsibility of good owners to make sure that it happens.

In too many cities, there is scant provision for walking dogs or perhaps there are burdensome 'leash laws' preventing them from running and associating with others. Dogs are not allowed to

small creatures in long grass and solve puzzles that you set during the walk.

For obvious reasons, dogs must be kept on a lead when being walked along roads or in other dangerous locations, and many of them hate it. Pulling on the leash, causing discomfort to both dog and walker, is the number-one complaint from dog owners, but it really need not be so. Early training should encourage a young dog to stay close beside you, feeling safer and more secure on a slack lead than pulling ahead on a tight one. Failure to train a puppy this way during the first few months of walking can create a life-time challenge. I have built a professional

PC finds my bed more attractive than sleeping on the floor or in his own space, but he cannot indulge in this luxury without my permission.

reputation on developing ways and means of stopping dogs from pulling, using accessories such as the Halti head collar and teaching alternative behaviours.

There is a host of dog-training accessories that rightly or wrongly claim to stop dogs pulling on the lead. More information about these and about leash training is provided in the next chapter.

Penalties

Life is not always a bed of roses for any of us and dogs need to live within a world of rules and expectations which complement our own. If as a child you played with electricity or touched a hot stove, you were punished. As an adult, if you run a red light, you expect to be prosecuted or killed. Similarly, penalties are essential to a balanced and pragmatic approach to dog training. Unruly and even unsafe behaviour such as jumping up, incessant barking, stealing food or chasing animals is simply unacceptable. A reward-based strategy alone cannot prevent these events from occurring. Here are some of my other methods for enforcing sensible ground rules.

Voice

My last book on dog training was called *Dog Training the Mugford Way: Never Say No!*. The purpose of the title was to discourage people from over-emphasizing the negative at the expense of the positive in dog training. But, of course, the word 'no' does have its place in our lexicon. There needs to be a signal that a particular activity should stop or at least that it is disapproved of. It does not have to be a word: the tone of voice, a hand signal or facial expression can be as or more effective.

The tone rather than content of our voices is the window to our emotional states. On this basis alone, dogs quickly come to recognize when we are calm, distressed, amused or angry, and respond accordingly.

Then there is the issue of intensity or loudness. Conversations with our dogs are best dealt with quietly. There should normally be no need to shout commands, given the superior hearing sensitivity of most dogs. However, there will be times and circumstances when a loud and angry voice is needed, such as when breaking up a fight. I have been a witness to too many dog fights and at the earliest beginnings of what may turn into a

The Scent Game

Locating objects by their scent is a fabulous game for so-called 'high-drive' dogs with particularly good sensory abilities, such as Spaniels or Border Collies. It can also make the walk a far more enjoyable prospect for an owner who may feel anxious about taking their 'high-drive' dog out. Make sure you have a favourite ball or other toy handy: playing with this will be the privilege to reward a successful find. Start the game by dropping an object such as a glove or a pebble and encourage the dog to 'go find' and retrieve. Allow a minute of play with the toy or ball, then repeat, throwing the object to be retrieved further and further into longer grass or over more difficult terrain. This is something that can start at home, or when the dog is having a moment of natural playfulness. This game worked wonders for Jez, a frustrated and sometimes very aggressive Jack Russell whom we were able to manage completely by providing fun search tasks. He could find a ball of grass which his owner had rolled in her hands, and later he even learned to track down a single blade of grass dropped in a field. Jez's walks became something more than just running and sniffing; they finally had a purpose for this demanding little terrier.

Jez's owner also benefited. He enjoyed the walk and setting the challenge of where to find the grass. It also enabled other members of the family to be able to interact with Jez, as he knew what was expected: the 'rules' of the game.

Labradors like Bounce were developed as gundogs, easily trained to retrieve birds during shoots. Find and fetch games exercise the same instinct – the pay-offs being just play and praise.

fracas, I holler, and holler loud! Practise making guttural, angry sounds with your voice, alone in a room with a mirror for company, where your dog can't hear you. Then use them on the dogs if something unacceptable is brewing.

'Ssh'

Another handy signal to interrupt unwanted behaviour is the 'ssh', as when releasing gas from a bottle of carbonated drink. This sound seems to have a generic significance for all manner of

---

Some Dos and Don'ts to Stop Dogs Pulling

- Do invest in a longer rather than a shorter lead. 2m (6ft 6in) is ideal. Two points of contact are much better than one.
- Do fit a comfortable harness and collar, so that you have two points of contact: on the dog's back and on his neck.
- Do stop frequently during walks, say every 15–20 paces. Reach down and stroke, speak and bond with the dog, wait a moment, then move on.
- Do carry treats so you can reward him for having his shoulders alongside your legs.
- Convention has it that dogs walk on your left. There is an old army tradition that you walk a horse on your left, carry a rifle in your right, and that convention was transferred to the world of dogs by the military. But if you really prefer walking a dog on your right, go ahead and dispense with tradition.

- Don't fit a choke chain, spike collar or other pain-inducing device. Remember that a dog's neck is as sensitive as yours is, so treat it with the same care.
- If you are failing, seek advice from a good dog trainer or other canine professional. It could be an important medical matter for both of you if a large dog pulled you into traffic or caused a muscle injury by pitching his strength against yours.
- Clicker training (see Chapter 4) can be a good way of targeting the non-pulling, walking-close response, but a softly spoken 'good boy' verbal reward is also effective.
- Use a double-ended lead attached to a collar, harness or head-collar.

The ideal outcome is for your dog to walk alongside your knee, with his lead slack. Pause every now and then in the 'sit' position. If he won't respond to you, seek advice from a canine professional.

Myth-Busting: Good Timing Is Helpful But Not Essential

Many authors and dog trainers will tell you that praise and certainly punishment must immediately follow the relevant behaviour. The problem with this approach is that it massively understates the cognitive ability of dogs. Unlike the rats and pigeons used in behavioural experiments, who were expected to perform relatively simple tasks such as pressing a bar, pecking at a key or jumping a barrier, dogs are capable of much more complex mental challenges that psychologists refer to as cognition. This is a form of thinking and of problem solving similar to the human use of intuition, trial and error and sometimes long-delayed symbolic reinforcements when dealing with complex situations. Dogs, and I expect many other animal species, seem to have mental capacities that are well beyond those explored and exploited by the early, laboratory-based learning theorists, and they are often understated by many dog trainers, even today.

The good news is that you can teach your dog important rules of behaviour that are linked to subtle gestures and expressions of approval or disapproval, using much more complex reinforcements than a titbit, a treat or an electric shock. These are exciting times in the world of animal learning, and your dog's mental abilities should cause you constant amazement. For instance, it is clear that dogs are capable of 'episodic memory', remembering a single event at a specific time and specific place, seemingly forever. Then we know that highly evolved primates, elephants, horses and even birds of the crow family are capable of social cognition. It has been shown experimentally that they can 'read the minds' of other individuals without reference to obvious gestures or body signals. I suspect that dogs can do the same when 'reading' us humans, in anticipation of our next move and of our emotions.

Dogs are capable of applying what psychologists call a fuzzy problem-solving strategy, making best-fit solutions to complex situations. This is good news for those of us trainers who have imperfect timing or don't want our dogs to behave like mechanical toys.

Remember, if you wouldn't train a child like a rat or a pigeon, don't use such harsh and simplistic methods on your dog!

Tricks such as 'shake hands' can be useful when distracting your dog from unwanted behaviour.

Develop your own set of signals to stop your dog stealing food. A flat hand signal combined with the 'ssh' sound works as a signal for Bubba.

creatures; my theory is that it relates back to the hiss signals from snakes, geese and a host of other potentially dangerous animals. It is a clear warning signal meaning 'Get away or else!'

You can make the ssh sound by expelling air through your teeth, by the well-timed release of gas from an aerosol or from one of the several designs of spray collars (see page 61). So practise your ssh and use it if your dog, say, picks up discarded garbage in the street or urine-marks a favourite shrub. It is the mildest of deterrents, but nevertheless a signal to stop.

Rattle Can

Earlier writers about dog training have suggested throwing a metallic object such as a bunch of keys or a choke chain to interrupt unwanted behaviours. The theory goes that the unexpected clatter will frighten the dog and cause him to desist. The theory is good enough, except that keys have sharp edges and most choke chains make a rather dull metallic thud when they land on the ground. Enter the rattle can or bottle!

This was one of my really good ideas that sadly cannot be patented, because all it needs is a couple of pebbles in a soft-drink can or bottle and, hey presto, you have a very effective interruptive stimulus.

It is important to understand that sensitive dogs can quickly learn to dislike the noise of

even a dislodged pebble, so be careful before exposing your dog to a rattle can. Monitor his sensitivity and adjust the intensity accordingly. However, for many dogs, it is a handy (and inexpensive) training aid. You can use it in all sorts of contexts: to stop a puppy stealing food from a low table, to discourage him from coming onto a sofa, going upstairs, chasing the family cat or rolling in fox excrement. If the context and timing are right, just drop the can within a metre (3ft) or so of the dog and say nothing. Is he surprised, amused (does he pick up the can as a plaything?), or is he frightened? He may be any or all of those things, but whatever his response he should be distracted from the unwanted behaviour. In no circumstances, however,

Dropping the rattle can nearby is enough to stop Buttons from eating something undesirable he has found in the grass.

should you allow him to play with the can, because it must not become a toy.

On second and subsequent occasions, you may have to toss the can harder or drop it more gently, depending on how he reacted the first time. But then I suggest that you immediately encourage him to come to you, to sit and be stroked or something else that he enjoys. Punishment of any sort leaves a vacuum that should be filled with desirable behaviours and positive karma.

Once the superstitious fear (by which I mean a fear that is disproportionately greater than the objective danger of a rattle can) has been formed, the slightest movement of a pebble within the can is sufficient to get the dog's attention and act as a substitute for that 'no' word. Overuse of a rattle can, or using it at the wrong time and/or in the wrong context, will undermine its effectiveness and could be harmful. Pretty soon, you should be able to phase it out and replace it with a gentler signal, such as the ssh sound.

Case Study: **Scooby the Sheep-Worrier**

Scooby is a confident, sociable Border Collie who came to me four years ago because he had joined in the activities of a terrier friend and killed many sheep. He didn't actively injure them, rather he herded them into a pile and those at the bottom suffocated: horrific suffering. Plainly this was a disaster and the farmer, not unreasonably, wanted the dogs to be killed. Instead, I offered Scooby a home and he is now an excellent working dog who has learned the limits of what he may and may not do with my sheep.

Scooby's initial preventative training relied upon simple or no-cost materials to hand on any farm: baler cord and pebbles in a can. We held him on a 10-metre (33ft) lead and walked him through my pet sheep; as he lunged in a playful manner, the can landed beside him. This happened four times, by which time our confident Scooby needed only a slight rattle to interrupt the earliest playful chase.

On the following day, we repeated the exercise and needed only one show of the can. After that Scooby never needed the warning again. He is now a delight to have on the farm and will perform a long down-stay even when our bottle-

fed pet lambs butt him or chew his ears. Scooby has learned the rules, but there had to be a well-timed and firm penalty for pursuing sheep.

Border Collies are the favourite choice for canine sports like agility and theme work to music, because they are tireless and attentive to minute sound and visual cues, as they have to be when working for a shepherd. But, they also make very demanding pets!

Border Collies instinctively herd sheep, but as my experience with Scooby shows it is possible to redirect this behaviour to more appropriate activities.

The rattle can is also effective in discouraging your dog from going upstairs without permission. 1 Put your dog in the 'stay' position. 2 When he attempts to climb the first step drop the can. 3 Continue to command 'stay' or 'down'.

The Wrong Approach to Training: Shock Collars

The technology for delivering electric shock to induce pain has evolved over half a century or more, from being conceived by dog trainers in Germany. Interestingly, use of shock collars is illegal in Germany nowadays, but elsewhere they are easily obtained. Industry estimates are that up to two million shock devices are sold worldwide every year to train dogs. They fall into three categories: those designed to fence a dog within his property and give a shock if he strays outside; those where a shock is activated by a radio signal from a transmitter held at a distance; and those that deliver a shock if the dog barks, triggered by an automated sensor within the collar.

Considerable controversy surrounds the use of all these devices and I personally would like to see them banned, because they cause dogs long-lasting emotional harm. In my view, they are a lazy and unreliable approach to training that does not acknowledge the complexity of dogs' emotions, their sensitive feelings or their ability

to learn. The biggest casualties from the use of shock collars are confidence and trust: a world that should be safe and interesting becomes dangerous to explore. I have seen this with my own dogs when they have been accidentally shocked by touching the electric fences used to contain sheep and cattle or to protect poultry and new-born lambs from predation by foxes. Then why, you might ask, is it OK to shock a sheep, cow or horse but not a dog?

Why Do Dogs and Cows React Differently to Shock Treatment?

Herbivorous herd animals like cattle and sheep exhibit high levels of vigilance, enabling them to detect then run away from danger, such as from wolves. Touching an electric wire creates a long-lasting fear of the fence, but cattle and sheep will graze up to and even under it. A single shock teaches them that only brief physical contact with a visible wire is dangerous.

Carnivores such as wolves or dogs are not as vulnerable to predation as herbivores. They also learn to avoid a visible stimulus such as wire, but develop a strong superstitious aversion to the place where the shock was experienced if there is no visible source or reason for the pain.

The high-tech shock collars sold for training dogs are, of course, invisible to the wearer once they are around his neck. There is no obvious warning sign or default option to receiving a shock. A dog may be shocked many times before he learns that crossing a boundary, barking or chasing deer is the cause of the pain. And believe me, these devices can be very painful: I have tried them out on myself. As an experiment, I suggest that you ask the person selling shock collars to try one on him or herself, preferably putting it around his neck and not on the less sensitive hand. There are very few fans of shock collars who will rise to that challenge!

collar which automatically releases a fine mist of gas in response to the dog's barking. Called the Aboistop (from the French aboyer: to bark), it instantly became a practical tool much favoured by canine professionals.

It also became known as the citronella spray collar because it was initially thought that incorporating citronella was necessary for the device to be unpleasant enough to stop a dog from barking. However, my observations suggest that the ssh noise alone is sufficient and that the scent of citronella remaining on the dog's coat is a punishment too far.

My experience is that the Aboistop, and similar products from other manufacturers, have a good level of success in reducing barking, but only if the barking is in response to threat

'A dog may be shocked many times before he learns that crossing a boundary or barking is the cause of the pain'

At time of writing, in the UK only the Welsh Parliament has passed legislation forbidding the sale of these collars. There seems little prospect of EU-wide legislation, and in the United States the shock-collar industry has a very powerful lobby among the hunting and working-dog fraternity. This is both an emotive and important issue about which I and other behaviourists and trainers hold strong views (mostly against). Don't do this to your best friend!

Spray Training

As I mentioned earlier, most dogs are highly sensitive to the 'ssh' sound because it seems to be one of nature's universal warning signals. The concept of having a collar that releases compressed gas – and therefore makes a ssh sound – was invented by a French veterinarian during the 1970s. Its first application was a

or disturbance: meaning territorial barking, which has a relatively low level of motivation. These devices don't usually work if the dog is barking because he is distressed at separation from companions or the human family, and indeed they may make an already anxious dog more frightened. Of course, as we shall read in Chapter 5, there are many different approaches to reducing or containing barking and we should focus upon the motives for the behaviour, not simply upon the noisy end symptoms.

A variation on the anti-bark spray collar is the radio-controlled spray collar, which can be activated by the owner or trainer via a hand-held transmitter. As with all aversive stimuli, this must always be delivered with good timing and in appropriate contexts. I find that the most useful application for this device is to interrupt predatory behaviour, such as dogs chasing after

Case Study: **Bella, the Deaf Dalmatian**

Deafness, which affects 2–3 per cent of all Dalmatians, is a controversial subject, with some people advocating that the animals should be euthanized at or as soon as possible after birth. In my view that is entirely wrong. Deafness in Dalmatians is an inherited condition and affected individuals should not be bred from. Particular care should also be taken that they do not run into danger, most obviously into traffic. But otherwise the disability can be readily accommodated and the deaf dog can experience a very good standard of life.

At my Behaviour Centre, we used a remote-controlled vibration collar to train Bella, who came to me as a highly obedient six-month-old, deaf, but well trained to recognize and obey hand signals. The purpose of the collar was to produce an orienting or 'Who goes there?' response, supported by a food reward. The approach to conditioning Bella was exactly the same as that used in clicker training (see page 70).

Bella was a fast learner and by the fifteenth vibration she was looking for her owners and then for the treat. That was two years ago, and Bella is now psychologically confined within a 100-metre (110-yard) radius, just inside the limit of the radio-control device. Technology can have benign applications for improving the lives of dogs.

sheep, cyclists and the like. We have also had good success using it to treat dogs that eat faeces (see Chapter 6).

Vibration Collars

Another application of technology in the service of dog training is to interrupt behaviour with the rattle or vibration of a device worn on the dog's collar. The reaction of individual dogs to this very mild sensation varies enormously. Many ignore it entirely, but if your dog is sensitive to it, it needs to be used thoughtfully and in

'The reaction of individual dogs to the very mild sensation of a vibration collar varies enormously'

appropriate circumstances, and not ever if it distresses him.

That said, vibration collars can be very useful for training deaf dogs (see box above).

Deaf dogs are
as easy to train as
any other, providing
the correct
equipment and
techniques are used.

4 Training Techniques

Relax! Training your dog is easy

Training Techniques

The right training for you and your dog. Attending classes or going it alone. Basic commands: sit-stay-come-heel. Clicker training and target training. Leash training, play training and scent training teach your dog to find your mobile when you can't. Problem solving and trick training.

Dogs are one of the easiest species on the planet to train, as long as we are empathetic and show patience towards them. Difficulties arise only when we are distracted from the task in hand and are inconsistent in the signals we give or the outcomes we expect. Fortunately, most dogs are clever enough to gloss over our mistakes in methodology and timing, making us look better trainers than we really are!

What Is Obedience?

You are right to want an obedient dog. However, what precisely do you mean by obedient? For many people, the word is defined by more than a dog knowing his name and coming when he is called. It entails the absence of a host of annoying behaviours, such as pulling on the lead, incessant barking, biting the postman or chasing joggers. My concept of obedience is that the dog's overall behaviour and attitude are nicely integrated with your lifestyle, he fulfils your reasonable expectations and he is compliant towards the usual signals of control. And, of course, I want him to be happy.

I propose this definition because it allows you to develop the habits and personality of your

'My concept of obedience is that the dog's overall behaviour and attitude is integrated with your lifestyle'

Training your dog is an anywhere and anytime activity, not just for dog school. A plentiful supply of treats helps!

dog, which might be different from anyone else's. Your dog may never respond to standardized commands like an automated zombie in an obedience competition, but you can work out the language and the signals of control that best work for the two of you.

Much of organized dog training can encourage exactly the opposite of my definition. There may be strict tests of compliance and grades of obedience promoted by the Kennel Club or other canine associations. To be fair, teaching a class of eight, ten or more dogs can force trainers to adopt a standardized approach, but that is not the theme of this book. For a variety of reasons, you may not want to attend training classes but would rather do it yourself, at home, where behaviour matters. However, one important benefit of attending group classes is that you meet other dogs and their people, making it a sociable outing for both of you. Social skills in dogs have to be learned and continuously developed.

Choosing a Trainer and a Training Class

It can be a challenge to find the trainer and the class that will be right for you and your pet. The only certain measure is a happy outcome and positive feedback from other owners, so take account of word-of-mouth recommendations and opinions expressed on the Internet.

Organizations

There are many bodies that accredit dog trainers with various levels of competence, but my experience is that some of the best trainers never join these organizations and may not boast impressive academic qualifications. Frankly, in the UK, US and perhaps everywhere, dog training is unregulated; anyone can invent spurious strings of letters behind their names – and many do. Too often, they mean nothing!

First Time

I recommend that you leave your dog at home the first time you go to a class, then watch and listen to what goes on before you commit to joining it. Is there a lot of shouting, barking and big dogs lunging at others, or does the trainer keep everyone happy and involved? Are there distractions that will interfere with your learning process? Check out the size of the class: of course small numbers are best, because the trainer's inputs will be diluted if there are too many other dogs.

Venue

The venue itself is also important. Dogs hate the slippery floors that many meeting halls have, and these places are often noisy. Outdoors is always best, but if indoors, look for non-slip surfaces such as can be found in a covered horse manege. Pet superstores are popular locations in the USA, but are far from ideal if they are noisy and there are the usual distractions of retail, smells of pet food and highly polished floors. However, there may be an opportunity to use car parks outside the store, which would resolve these problems.

From the age of six weeks a puppy will instinctively follow you if you move away. 1 Call him as he follows you to help him get used to his name. 2 Reward him for following you.

When Should Training Begin?

A puppy starts learning as soon as his senses begin to function, so from two to three weeks of age. He can express preferences for warm over cold, sweet over sour, and he will have developed a keen sense of smell to guide him towards his mother's nipples. Success in these tiny life-defining skills encourages him to explore the world around him and fills a memory bank of what are hopefully mostly positive experiences, but with some to be avoided because they were unpleasant. This is the beginning of the 'payoffs versus penalties' attitude to life, which is my guiding principle to dog training.

Myth-Busting: Training Theory

It used to be thought that dogs should do what we want them to do because they feel obliged to 'please' their master. This was the so-called compulsive training method, where a yank or 'check' on the collar, a stern word or, worse, a whack would be delivered if the dog did the 'wrong' thing or failed to respond to a command. Of course, this approach is a nonsense – would we teach our children that way? Thankfully there are very few of the diehard compulsive punishers left, because there has been a massive swing in fashion and practice towards reward-based methods.

I will be extolling the virtues of clicker training (see page 70) throughout this book, but it should not be seen as the only or even the best way to go about dog training. The simple words 'Good boy' quickly become embedded in the dog's mind as indicating the 'right' way forward. For discouragement or to signal 'stop doing that', you could say 'No!', but I would rather recommend the 'ssh' sound (see page 56).

Uttered through clenched teeth, this is a very effective aversive stimulus, so long as the context (unwanted behaviour) is exactly right.

First Steps

Good breeders begin training puppies as soon as they can focus on humans as opposed to litter mates and mother. The easiest response to teach is 'follow', associated with the 'come' command. A puppy's natural tendency to follow is strongest at about six weeks of age. Walk away from him when there are no distractions and he should follow; as he does, say the word 'come'. The very act of following strengthens a puppy's imprint on people, which is vital for later training.

Studies have shown that gentle handling of puppies, almost from day one, accelerates their neurological and sensory development. Another benefit of this hands-on approach is that the puppies become imprinted to the smell and later the sight and sounds of humans, treating us as though we were one of them. This is the ultimate in socialization of puppies, ensuring that they will be trusting and responsive towards people.

If you adopt a puppy between the later ages of 8 and 12 weeks and the breeder did not make these early handling investments, then formal 'come' and 'follow' training should be your first priority. It is always best to precede any such training with the dog's name, so, 'Rover – come!'

Classical Conditioning versus Instrumental Learning

Scientists have long been studying animals and how they learn. Some of the best known experiments were conducted in the early 20th century by the Russian physiologist Ivan Pavlov, who showed that dogs learn to anticipate the arrival of something pleasant such as food by salivating; they will also react in advance to an unpleasant event such as an electric shock if it is reliably preceded by a buzzer. This is called classical conditioning and it is very relevant to our understanding of the behaviour of pet dogs.

Of course, I don't expect you to wire your dog up in the rather unpleasant fashion of Pavlov's laboratory. Your day-to-day activities will have conditioned your dog to a whole array of stimuli. Your actions to prepare and offer food are exactly along the lines of Pavlov's experiments: the dog is conditioned to your gestures and salivates in anticipation. When you put on outdoor clothes before going for a walk, you trigger emotional responses such as excited barking. Here, the conditioned stimulus is your wearing of outdoor clothes, the conditioned response is excitement in anticipation of a walk.

Instrumental learning, also referred to as operant conditioning, plays a big part in everyday dog behaviour and learning. Your dog is actually instrumental in devising payoffs and penalties for himself. For instance, by amusing you with a bow or offering a paw, a clever dog finds that he can elicit a reciprocal, friendly response from you. You like to see him happy so you approach him, praise him and give him a treat. Here, the dog is managing your behaviour, producing a pleasant outcome for himself.

Training Never Stops

Everything you do with your dog has an effect upon his subsequent behaviour. You may think that training is just for formal classes and that what happens in between doesn't matter. In reality, every moment and activity give you an opportunity to train your dog, or for him to learn things that you would rather he did not.

Consistency is the key to training a young dog, but as they mature they become able to deal with changes to the rules of the game or even to the rules being reversed. It is remarkable that more dogs don't become confused, neurotic creatures. They are well able to work out our intentions by factoring in the context of our behaviour, guessing what it is that you want them to do.

Clicker Training

This came into popularity when American trainers were teaching dolphins to perform tricks in the likes of Disney World. For our purposes, it relies upon delivering a clear, simple click sound at the precise moment a dog is seen to perform the 'right' action, associating the click with the behaviour. The click itself has no significance unless it is first paired with the offering of a treat or reward.

Clickers are cheap and come in a variety of shapes and sizes, but the principle is always the same: they produce a sound that will not be confused with any other noise. You could use your voice to say 'Good boy' in the same context, but the outcome would be less precise because the human voice is fuzzy and variable, whereas a click is not. As an alternative to using a clicker, you could click with your tongue or fingers.

To begin using a clicker in training, start with something simple like a 'lie down' response.
1 Be ready with your clicker for your dog beginning to adopt the traditional sphinx pose.
2 Wait until the dog spontaneously adopts the classic sphinx posture and link it to the 'down' command and a clear hand-gesture.
3 Click, then praise and/or reward your dog.

Target Training and the Use of Lures

Training your dog to follow the end of a stick or 'wand' with his nose will give you lots of extra training 'power', with him ultimately performing new and more demanding tasks. Target sticks can be purchased or home-made from a short cane with a wine cork on the end. The first stage is to have the dog approach and sniff a meat-smeared cork, then click and treat. Repeat several times until your dog associates touching the cork with a rewarding outcome, then slowly move the now clean cork that he must follow to obtain the payoff of a click and treat.

Soon, you will be able to lure your dog towards an object you want him to pick up on command, to follow between your legs as part of a dance routine or to 'go to your basket'. This technique is used nowadays by professional trainers who need dogs to perform really complex tasks such as opening doors for wheelchair users, guiding the blind away from obstructions or fetching a pouch containing life-saving medicines for a diabetic owner. However, you can use a target stick to simply have fun together and improve your control during sports such as agility, heelwork to music or searching for objects by their scent. Once the dog has

Once you have trained your dog to follow a target stick you will be able to teach him a range of complex and useful tasks.

learned to follow the stick, these complex training scenarios become possible.

In the same way you can link any number of spontaneously performed movements or gestures to simple word commands, hand, body and facial signals. If you watch the performance of skilled trainers who, say, perform at the top level in heelwork to music, you will notice a rapid succession of subtle body, facial and voice signals by which the trainer controls the artistry of his dog.

Dogs easily learn to respond to hand signals which mean anything from 'come' or 'fetch' to 'get in the car'.

The Essential Four Commands: Sit-Stay-Come-Heel

These are the four basic control responses that every dog needs to know, and the earlier they are taught the better. None of them are difficult if you go about it the right way, though if you have an untrained adult dog you may need more specialized techniques and accessories than I describe here.

'Sit'

When the puppy or dog spontaneously sits, you should always give the 'sit' command. 'Click' if you are using clicker training, then restate 'sit' and reward him when he obeys. A forward-facing flat of hand can be a useful signal for this, supplemented by the 'stay' or 'wait' command.

1 Hold a titbit in your hand, then lift it to just above his head, luring him backwards … 2 … until he slips into the sit posture. 3 The moment he does, open your hand to give the reward. Only in rare circumstances is the treat really necessary; often it is better to use the instrumental learning method, with or without a clicker.

Hand signals

Dogs are more attentive to visual signals than to our voice, so it is sensible to combine the two. This Cattle dog is deaf, so hand signals are a must.

1 Show the flat of hand as a signal for 'stay'. 2 'Good boy' can be signified with thumbs up, and to release him from the 'sit'. 3 Arms outstretched is a good signal for come.

'Stay'

I was once a judge in a mass sit competition where one trusting Border Collie stayed in a sit-stay for an hour, after which time we all became bored and declared him the worthy winner!

1 Begin by putting your dog into a sit posture. 2 Command 'wait' or 'stay'. 3 Stand back. 4 After just a few seconds, reward him and release him from sit. Repeat the procedure but extend the duration before offering a reward. Try to achieve a one-minute stay before treating.

When It Goes Wrong – Sit and Stay

Should you tether a dog in this stay exercise? That may seem like a cheating short cut, but for a dog who doesn't understand that 'sit-stay' means 'do not move', it can be an aid to training. If you are having difficulties training your dog to stay, try tethering him to a tree or some such firm point and gradually lengthen the period of stay, rewarding at each significant milestone.

Maybe your dog has jumped to his feet as you stepped away. If that happens, return immediately, reiterate the 'sit-stay' command but do not reward him. Repeat the step away for a shorter distance and for less time. You are aiming to reward only a successful, tolerated

'sit-stay'; the 'punishment' for his non-compliance is for the reward to be withheld. Do not reprimand or in any other way directly punish him. It is possible that he is reluctant to remain in a 'sit-stay' posture because he is overly

What Not to Do

There is one way not to teach a dog to sit, and that is to yank his neck on the collar or choke chain, then push his bottom down with the other hand. That is the bad old compulsive way and will very likely make the poor dog afraid of your hands. Don't do it!

'Come'

If your dog hasn't been trained to follow at an early age (see page 69), you may have to resort to more structured training methods. If he has a tendency to run away or does not respond to his name or 'come', do your initial training in an escape-proof setting, such as an enclosed tennis court or fenced garden.

1 Command your dog to 'sit' and 'stay', then move back a few paces. 2 Link the 'come' command to an open arms gesture by calling 'Rover, come.' (Remember, it's good to link any commands to his name.) The chances are that he will come, especially if you are carrying treats. 3 Tempt him with the rustle of a food wrapper, treat bag or toy, then when he comes and has dropped into a sit posture, reward him.

'Come' using a house line

Some dogs are headstrong and do not respond to 'come'. You will need the help of a competent trainer, working in a safe and enclosed space, such as a tennis court, where compliance can be made compulsory, but still rewarded.

1 When the puppy or dog spontaneously sits, give the 'sit' command.
2 'Click' (if you are using clicker training), then restate 'sit'. 3 … and reward him.

When It Goes Wrong – Come

Some dogs prefer freedom to human company and will run and run into danger, justifying a more structured training approach. Use high-value treats (pay-off) and wait for the moment the dogs makes eye contact or walks towards you: signal 'come' and reward. Repeat. In difficult cases I sometimes use a radio-controlled spray collar (penalty) to interrupt.

When It Goes Wrong – Heel

Too many of us have dogs that walk very well to heel when there are no distractions, but pull ahead if they see a cat or squirrel to chase, other dogs to compete with or because they are just naturally enthusiastic. Rather than near-garrotting the dog by 'checking' on his collar, I recommend the luring technique of carrying a treat to focus his attention and keep him close as you walk ahead. From time to time, stop, put him into a sit and treat. It was for powerful dogs like Charli that I invented the Halti head collar which provides a short term solution whilst developing a longer term training strategy.

'Heel'

You have probably found that whereas you are a walker, your dog is more of a runner! It must be really irritating for dogs having to slow down to our 3–5 km (2–3 miles) per hour walk when their natural pace is nearer 15–30 km (10–20 miles) per hour. Nevertheless, it's something they have to do, and they mostly have to do it on a lead.

1 The easy way to teach a dog to walk close beside you or to heel is with a clicker, clicking and rewarding him each time he is within, say, a 1–2 m (3–6ft) range. 2 As training progresses, reward him only for being closer and closer, until he eventually positions himself just opposite your knees and walks by you in a straight line.

• You can achieve the same result by training the puppy on a slack lead, ideally one of about 2m (6ft 6in). This allows him to deviate and walk outside the target 'close zone', so that he will learn that he is rewarded only when he is inside it and near to you.

Case Study: **Humphrey the Persistent Puller**

There are some dogs whom no amount of reward-based training will stop from trying to forge ahead. I have one such dog, Humphrey, who becomes a carthorse the moment he feels tension on the lead. One approach with a persistent puller like him is to use a longer lead, at least a 2m (6ft 6in) conventional one or perhaps an extending lead of the Flexi type. Let the dog move forward and outside the target 'close zone', then turn back on yourself so that he has to follow rather than move ahead of you. Repeat this a few times and (hopefully) he will learn that the quickest way of travelling from A to B is not to pull. You can, if you are dexterous, make a click sound with an extending lead with the brake button on the plastic body. This can be a good substitute for the conventional 'heel' command.

For instance, a sweeping hand gesture behind an open car door can mean 'Get in', whereas the same gesture in a park may mean 'Go fetch a toy.' Dogs soon learn to understand the nuances of our commands and gestures.

'Stop Pulling' Accessories

The Halti, which is perhaps the world's best-known design of head collar, is my invention and was inspired by my having spent a lifetime among horses. I just scaled down halters of

Fitting a Halti

The first Halti experience for a dog must be rewarding to compensate for the strangeness of wearing a head collar. I recommend this sequence for fitting any design of head collar.

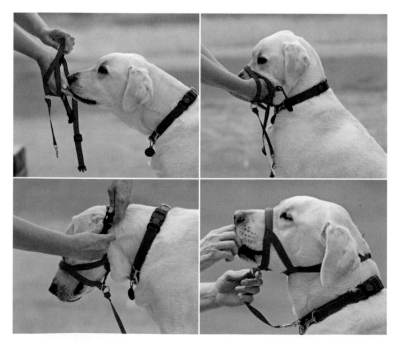

1 Hold a high-value treat in front of the dog through the Halti.
2 Give him the treat as you slip the Halti over his nose.
3 More treats, then adjust the neck/collar section and fasten the buckle.
4 Fit the safety link to the D-ring of his collar, then check that the size and adjustments are correct with the nose-piece well away from his eyes. More treats! Attach a light lead to the head collar, then slowly walk him with more treats, then praise for tolerance.

Putting on a Front Control Harness

Designs such as the Halti harness and the Easy Walk are another effective means of stopping a dog from pulling and are often better accepted by them than head collars.

1 Slip the harness over the head and adjust the straps to suit the dog.
2 Fasten the belly strap and adjust to a snug fit.
3 Link the harness to his collar so the front strap rides above his legs and does not interfere with his walking.
4 Fit a double-ended lead to fronts and back, to give more precise steering control.

the kind that have been used for thousands of years on horses, cattle, camels and llamas, then adjusted the construction so that it would fit comfortably on a dog's face. Like all head collars, it works on the principle that if you direct an animal's head, its body has to follow.

Head collars have revolutionized less able owners' prospects for walking strong dogs. No harsh checking from the owner is required and the dog soon learns that his walks will be most comfortable if they are conducted on a slack lead.

There are now many designs of canine head collar available and most are very effective at stopping dogs from pulling ahead. However, my view remains that they are best used as an interim training tool, not as a permanent solution. With your dog wearing his head collar, use the clicker principles outlined earlier so he learns that the best place to walk is beside you.

Harnesses

Harnesses are a kind way of distributing physical force over wide areas of a dog's body, rather than localizing it on his neck. Many encourage pulling, as for sledge or guide dogs; however, some designs should reduce the amount of pulling ahead a dog does and perhaps even prevent it altogether. There are two categories of anti-pulling harnesses: those that compress or cause pain when the dog pulls, and those that act as a steering device by having a point of control on the thorax or front of the dog.

Front-control harnesses are my preferred solution, where two points of attachment can be connected to a double-ended lead and you can steer the dog from either his chest or his collar. This can be a very gentle but reliable way of achieving complete control of an otherwise over-boisterous and unresponsive, pulling dog.

Myth-Busting: There's No Need for Spike Collars and Choke Chains

There have been many inventions intended to stop dogs pulling. Some of them are harmless and effective (see main text), but some are quite awful in the way they work. Still popular in some countries is the spike collar, whose inward-facing sharp metal wires press upon the sensitive structure of the throat, discouraging the dog from pulling. Unfortunately, such devices can cause injuries to the neck and they must undermine the trust that should exist between man and dog out for a walk together.

Another horror is the choke chain that tightens around a dog's neck like a hangman's noose and, despite its obvious welfare drawbacks, is employed by many dog trainers. If they are used in the recommended way, a skilled trainer delivers two or more harsh 'checks' and, in theory, the pain the dog experiences quickly conditions him to stop pulling. The trouble is that choke chains are widely sold in pet stores with no instructions on how they should be used. Inevitably, most owners do not have the strength or skill to make those first, painful 'checks', so the dog carries on pulling, closing off his windpipe. There are numerous cases of dogs fainting and of whiplash injuries caused by over-vigorous yanking on the lead. Choke chains should be banned from open sale.

Play-Training

Play provides practice in survival skills for both people and animals. That your dog wants to play is a measure of his wellbeing: he is in a good mood, so consider it a compliment. Play is one of the primary motivators and reward systems for dogs, and you should nurture this side of his character. If you don't want to join in his games,

maybe you should keep houseplants and not this sentient animal.

Play between you and your dog is fine so long as, at some point, you can dictate the rules of the game. It may be that your dog has to come, sit, 'give me a paw' and then have the ball thrown to complete a fetch sequence. With tug-of-war games it must be you who determines when the

Play has two elements: that directed towards other dogs and people (social play) and that involving toys, sticks or other accessories (object play). Sometimes the two cross over, with you being invited to chase your dog because he has found a marvellous toy, and roles reverse when you catch up and are able to gain possession of his treasure.

When your dog has learned to find a sock or other object in a cardboard box, make the task harder by putting the box into another box, then another and so on like Russian dolls.

'battle' is over, and the dog must give up final possession of the object to you.

There is a fantastic variety of dog toys in your local pet store and most of them are just great, but a few may be dangerous because they are small enough for your dog to swallow. Check out toys for toughness and watch your dog at all times when he is playing with something new. If he has shredded it into loose, potentially hazardous bits, remove and discard it.

The best games are those that require a combination of physical skill and mental or problem-solving ability. One is tracking, another is working at social or interactive games.

that the dog has to use his nose and all his other senses to locate it.

The reward for each successful find can be as big as you want to make it, such as a session with his favourite squeaky toy, a tug-of-war game or anything that excites and maintains his motivation to search.

Scent Trails

Following a scent trail is another easy and fun task to teach your dog. Begin by having a member of the family or friend walk away and be seen to hide behind a tree or some other such hideaway. Send the dog to 'find him'. Give him a

'I once knew a collie who had a search memory for 90+ items, so he could be sent to retrieve specific toys'

Tracking and Nose Work

Dogs have, as we know, a remarkable olfactory sense that can be harnessed for both fun and function. Start with the easy task of hiding an item like a worn (that is, smelly) sock somewhere obvious like under the carpet, and reward the dog for pulling it out and bringing it to you. Then make it harder: change the item to, say, a rolled ball of grass that you throw onto the lawn or in a field. Make the ball smaller and smaller but the area to be searched larger and larger so

reward, or have the person he has found do so. Then make the distance travelled and the terrain to be crossed increasingly difficult, so the dog is faced with the challenge of having to use his nose, eyes and ears to find the missing person.

Tracking and nose work are no longer activities just for professionals; rather they are becoming increasingly popular canine sports. And from time to time, a trained search dog can help you out when, as I often do, you lose a bunch of keys, a wallet or mobile phone.

Pre-train your dog by showing it your phone (or your keys, shoes or whatever you are prone to losing), saying, 'Mobile', then hiding it in another room. Say, 'Go fetch the mobile' and reward him when he does. Repeat the exercise a few more times and your dog will have become a really useful object-finder.

I once knew a collie who had a search memory for 90+ items, so he could be sent to retrieve specific dog toys, his rather than her shoes, and so on. Unfortunately, our Labrador Bounce can remember only six such items; his fault or mine?

Interactive Games

Play need not just involve the physical side of a dog's character, but should also tax his mental or problem-solving abilities. An English Victorian peer, Lord Lubbock, trained his Poodle, Van, to recognize and associate quite complex words and symbols with particular rewards. If he was hungry, Van would spontaneously bring the cut out words 'feed me' to his master. Our dogs just bring us their food bowls!

Another famously clever dog was Fellow, the pet of Jacob Herbert from Detroit. Jacob had always talked to his dog as if he were a child and Fellow could respond accurately to many commands, such as 'Look up at the squirrel' or 'Go find my gloves.' This proved that Fellow could not only understand words, but that he could also remember interesting groups of words, to the extent of recognizing them in an appropriate syntactical context. However, to put the cognitive abilities of dogs into perspective, they are never quite as clever as Washoe, the famous chimpanzee who died in 2007; he had been taught by American scientists to use 250 sign language 'words', and made combinations of signs as might a deaf person in conversation.

Problem-Solving Games

There is a wealth of such games that you can, with a little imagination, use to test your dog's memory and cognitive ability. One simple approach is to hide a treat under one of three cups, then move them about while the dog is watching. Does he go to the 'correct' cup first or is he confused by your moving them?

Then, you can test his colour sensitivity by rewarding the cup that bears a red spot rather than the one with a blue or yellow spot. You can explore shape discrimination with the same set of cups, making fine distinctions between a circle and two ellipses or a triangle and two polygons.

This cunning food dispenser is a great way to test your dog's cognitive ability. When he works out which cover to press or slide, he will discover a food treat hidden underneath.

Play dead! This trick is best taught when your dog already lies down for a reward. 1 When your dog is in a 'sit' position, hold two fingers out as if a pretend gun. 2 When he lies down, 'click'. 3 Extend the trick by luring him to roll over, click and treat again.

The art and practice of testing and stimulating dogs' abilities to solve problems has been made available in a practical way to ordinary dog owners by Nina Ottosson, a Swedish trainer with an inventive approach to designing board games for dogs. She has produced a vast array of designs that require dogs to use their paws, nose and memory and all to obtain a small titbit reward. Importantly, Nina's games (and there are other manufacturers) require owners to participate and set the rules of the game – otherwise too many dogs would cheat by just picking up the board and shaking it!

Trick Training

Dogs love to perform tricks, be it 'give me a paw/give me five', 'roll over', play 'dead', 'speak' on command, sit up and beg (not always good for dogs with weak spines) and so on. Some tricks might seem humiliating and are best avoided unless you plan to form a private circus. However, reward-based trick training using clickers and allied to the principles of instrumental conditioning are just fine, will impress your friends and amuse the dog. Remember, they never stop learning, not even in old age.

To Sum Up

So much of dog training has been brought into disrepute by seeming to be allied with harsh methods and painful equipment such as shock collars, spike and choke chains. You now realize that none of this is necessary. Better results are obtained from the rustle of a treat packet, a gentle voice, a favourite squeaky toy and, as a punishment, either withdrawal of something he likes or that 'ssh' sound which he dislikes, but never physical violence. The most important outcomes from dog training happen in your own home, but if you enjoy the social goings-on of a training club, your dog will certainly also benefit from being in the company of other dogs. And like parents after kindergarten, you can boast about just how talented your dog is compared to theirs!

Bulldogs in particular love anything to do with wheels. I recommend that you feed rather than fight the habit, and Star is now a very accomplished skate-boarder.

5 Training Challenges

Why does he keep doing that?

Training Challenges

Those annoying quirks: jumping up, urine-marking, stealing food and other bad habits. They may not be serious, but they may annoy your non-dog-loving friends and it's worth learning to control them. Payoffs and penalties come in useful again, as do counter-conditioning and response substitution training.

The previous chapter dealt with basic obedience, showing how to exert control over your dog for his protection in a dangerous world. This chapter shows you how to stop him indulging in 'bad habits'. It is natural to want your dog to be fun and to be different from other dogs. However, there are some eccentricities you would rather be without: screaming like a banshee in the car or finding a thrill in mating cushions, urine-marking against an antique sofa or jumping up with mucky paws at the one person who happens not to be a dog lover.

Counter-Conditioning

Dealing with such behavioural challenges used to be described as 'corrective training' and tended to focus upon inflicting unpleasantness and even pain to 'correct' these so-called misbehaviours. However, most can be dealt with by the application of brains rather than brawn, by counter-conditioning or 'response substitution' training. This approach is based on creating new and desirable responses that compete with or substitute for the unwanted ones.

Just as a good parent has to set boundaries to their child's behaviour by applying such penalties

'Jumping up is too often inadvertently trained by owners who haven't thought through the consequences'

Jumping up is a classic candidate for response substitution training, where 'Sit!' is the alternative to unwanted jumping. You want your dog to greet you and to be friendly towards others, but if he jumps up, step back so that he is jumping into space.

as cancelling a fun trip, closing down the Internet or withholding money, so dog owners may also have to apply sanctions as a penalty for certain unacceptable behaviours. It could be the time for tough love! We all have different needs and expectations from our dogs and what I might tolerate you could find unacceptable. For instance, I am not bothered that my dogs eat dung on the farm, but disapprove of their touching faeces from foxes or other dogs. You may prefer your dog to do neither of these things. What follows is a gazette of irritations which may or may not be relevant to you and your dog. None is so serious as to be called a behavioural problem; rather they are normal canine traits that we would rather be without.

Jumping Up

You may be flattered that a puppy jumps up to be petted; you probably even let him lick your face. But the puppy that can only jump to knee height will soon grow into a dog that can reach above the waist and splatter muddy paws over clothes. More seriously, dogs that jump up are a major cause of injuries to old people who are unsteady on their feet and liable to fall and fracture bones. All in all, jumping up is too often inadvertently trained by owners who perceive it as cute and haven't thought through the consequences, or have not been consistent in teaching the dog an alternative way of greeting humans.

Penalties

Having established the rewarded alternative to jumping up, what might be the penalty if your dog continues to perform a full-on body slam when he greets people?

If the modest penalty of stepping back so that he jumps into empty space doesn't stop him, the next, more severe one would be to drop a noisy object such as a rattle can (see page 58). Your timing must be good, which means you must be prepared with your rattle device in advance. Then, once again, command the 'sit' response.

For some dogs, the rattle of a few pebbles in a can is not quite scary enough: they are just as likely to pick it up and use it as a plaything. For those dogs, we have the ssh noise of a Pet Corrector (see page 89).

Urine-Marking

Dogs mark out their territory by leaving urine for others to read, so that they can recognize who passed by and when. Thanks to the make-up of their urine, male dogs can be distinguished

Myth-Busting: You Don't Need to Use Force

I have dusted off my large collection of old-time and discredited dog-training books, which propose one or more of the following cruel methods to discourage jumping up:

• knee the dog sharply in the belly
• tread on his hind feet
• squeeze his forepaws
• spray with pepper
• check or yank his choke chain
• zap with a shock collar

This scary litany of torture is all found in books written in the last 20 years. The sad truth is that the authors failed to acknowledge why dogs want to jump up. It is exactly what they do when they meet another dog: sniff heads and tails, lick lips – the canine equivalent of greeting with a handshake, a hug or a kiss on the cheek. You shouldn't be responding to this sort of behaviour with harsh treatment that your dog won't understand.

The Pet Corrector is yet another way of turning a dog's natural aversion to the 'ssh' sound to good effect in your training programme.

Greeting ceremonies are important to dogs, so contact and licking after a time apart is essential to maintaining a trusting relationship.
1 Spend time teaching a reliable 'sit' response to an up-turned hand signal.
2 When he responds, reward him with a treat or let him play with his favourite toy. Bend down and stroke his head and muzzle, letting him sniff and lick your hands.

Getting Rid of Stains and Smells

Removing all the complex chemicals that are contained in a dog's urine is a challenge for any household cleaner. It is best to use brands that have a biological action, because they contain either enzymes or ammonia-digesting microbes. Complete the cleaning process with an alcohol (methylated spirits) swab, to remove fatty residues that weren't taken up in the water-detergent mix. The smell from residual urine stains can be awful because they harbour gas-forming bacteria. A benign (ie. non-toxic) range of antimicrobial products has just been launched under the Biotrol label, which I have found to be very effective at removing the odours associated with dog urine.

from bitches, castrated males from entire ones and bitches by their stage of oestrus ('heat' or 'season'). The frequency of urine-marking increases dramatically when a bitch is in season and males can pick up her scent from up to 20km (12 miles) away in open country. No one has done the research to determine if city dogs can follow a scent to source as well as their country cousins, but it would be a dangerous game for urban dogs to follow the smell of a bitch in season through city traffic.

The frequency of urine-marking in males is also under hormonal control, specifically by testosterone. Castration reliably reduces the motivation to urine-mark but does not entirely eliminate it. In other words, castrated dogs will still urinate against lampposts and, regrettably, even mark a friend's favourite sofa. What can be done to discourage this?

Consider the behavioural ecology of urine-marking. Take your dog for walks along defined routes and allow him to sniff the marks of other dogs and to 'cover' them with his own urine. Many owners try to drag their dogs away

The Pet Corrector

This handy device creates a mix of high- and low-frequency hisses by means of the sudden release of an inert gas across an aerofoil. When you use it, point it away from the dog.

Individual dogs react to the Pet Corrector in markedly different ways. Some are genuinely frightened and you should not use it on them. At the other extreme, some barely respond at all: it is as if they were deaf (and some may well be deaf to high-frequency sounds). Fortunately, about 90 per cent of dogs do respond to the hiss as a benign 'no' signal, a minor penalty to be avoided.

In training you will probably have to use a Pet Corrector only two or three times. Thereafter, hold it in your top pocket and let the dog see that it might be the penalty-in-waiting for jumping up. Then give the 'sit' command.

from lampposts, fire hydrants or trees, but this is unfair because urine carries important information that your dog wants to receive. Consider praising him for depositing urine marks on top of other dogs' messages outdoors, which will make him less likely to mark indoors.

At home, you probably want to draw a clear distinction between urine-marking inside the house (forbidden) and outside (perfectly all right). Unfortunately, some dogs fail to make this distinction, perhaps because they feel insecure in

'Many owners try to drag their dogs away from lampposts, fire hydrants or trees, but this is unfair'

the home and have picked up the scents of other canine visitors. If that happens, it is best to not allow other dogs into your home but encourage them to visit the garden. Multi-dog households that include both sexes are more likely to have the male urine-marking, especially if the female is in season. The way forward may be to spay her or to castrate him.

Stealing Food

Most dogs have a moral sense of what is 'right' and 'wrong'. Unfortunately, there are exceptions to these finely drawn distinctions and some dogs will steal food from the table with no apparent sense of remorse or guilt. How do you teach morality to a dog? The first priority is for him to learn the difference between foods intended for humans and those meant for dogs. This is a distinction that should have been established in puppy days, but if it was not, it's never too late to learn. Do not feed him at the table on

Dogs often urine-mark because they feel insecure in the home. If this happens, keep visiting dogs in the garden so that they don't leave their scent indoors.

Training a dog to go to a mat or favourite place out of the way of temptation can be a useful tactic for many situations, including preparing your dog's food and greeting visitors.

Use clicker training, to train him to leave your food alone. When he passes food on the table click and treat to reward him for leaving it, never with food from the plate.

If he continues to be distracted by your food discourage this behaviour with a firm hand signal coupled with a pet corrector, later substituted with the hand signal alone.

human-style snacks or leftovers from your meals. If you have children, train them not to drop crisp packets and other snack foods where the dog can steal them. This is a good opportunity to bring back the traditional notion of a sit-down family meal and divert the dog into an alternative activity such as chewing a bone or emptying a food-dispensing Kong or other such toy.

Stealing food is a perfect training model for the payoffs and penalty regime in dogs, just as it is used to discourage criminal theft by people. On the payoffs side, it is possible to apply clicker training principles to reward a dog for not stealing food. Put a plate of leftover human food on an accessible surface and, as your dog walks past it, click and treat. But make sure you use a dog treat and not a human food item.

As a penalty, be prepared to intervene with a stern 'No!' or to ambush him as he begins his career in crime with an aversive noise such as the rattle can, the Pet Corrector or the 'ssh' sound through clenched teeth.

My clients have given me some fantastic anecdotes about their dogs consuming gargantuan quantities of stolen human foods, such as the Sunday roast or the Christmas turkey. People have come home to find the freezer

door open with contents scattered and nibbled by a very sick dog. A moment's distraction to answer the door or take a phone call and Rover leaps to clear the table. In any such situation, don't 'blame' the dog, nor directly punish him. Taking food was massively rewarding for him, so punishment out of context will not have any meaning; worse, it will destroy his trust in you.

Sex

I expect dogs enjoy having sex as much as we do, but most owners disapprove of their pet becoming too amorous towards a pillow or someone's leg. The first priority is to castrate if he's a male and to monitor whether a bitch's errant sexuality correlates with her stage of oestrus. If that is the case and she is only over-sexed just before coming into season, there may be persuasive grounds for having her spayed.

But what if the sexual behaviour continues after neutering? Dogs have the same pleasure centres on their sexual organs as we do and the agreeable sensation of stimulating the penis or the clitoris may not be eradicated by removing the key sexual hormones. Sexual mounting is a normal part of juvenile play and continues into adult life, even in neutered males; they may even successfully copulate with bitches in season. Our young, castrated Labrador Bounce once tried to mount his best friend, who is a bottle-reared pet lamb. He was duly reprimanded: sex between a dog and sheep is just not acceptable to us traditional types!

So how can we divert or discourage dogs from having sex with humans, lambs or any other such innocents? The first priority should be to remove temptation: take away the cushions and don't sit in a way that you know, from past experience, invites your dog's unwelcome attention. Distract and redirect him into other activities such as searching for and fetching a toy or emptying a food-dispensing toy at the moment you see the tell-tale amorous signs developing. You have to be consistent, not crossing your legs on an easy chair and allowing him to mate today but not tomorrow. It is all or nothing when it comes to having consensual sex with a dog!

The penalty for unwanted sex must be immediate and meaningful to the dog. Ideally, it should not involve you touching him, since

'How can we discourage dogs from having sex with humans, lambs or any other such innocents?'

that will reinforce the very behaviour you want to suppress. Better to deliver a remote, surprise stimulus such as a water spray or the Pet Corrector 'ssh' sound. Never strike or physically hurt your oversexed dog, but rather remind yourself that he has been socialized towards both people and dogs, so either could be an acceptable sexual partner in his humanized mind.

Rolling in Muck

It is a too common experience that, when we take dogs to the woods, they find a spot that holds their attention for longer than usual, their eyes glaze over and then they roll in something awful – a maggoty dead crow, a putrid decaying fungus or, even worse, fox faeces.

Rolling in something pungent is a behaviour dating back to the days when confusing a predator was an important survival tactic. Just as human hunters dress in camouflage and even apply special animal perfume to avoid detection, so your dog chooses to adopt a smelly chemical disguise. It seems to be so deeply ingrained that even turning a cold hose on my dogs doesn't deter them.

What can be done to stop this unpleasant behaviour? Well, I have researched the subject for 30 years and conclude … not very much! It is, unfortunately, something that dogs do and you just have to carry a deodorizing dry shampoo, then divert to a dog-grooming parlour. I wash my farm dogs under a cold outdoor hose and you would think that the punishment of a cold shower might put them off doing it again. But it never does!

Nuisance Barking

There is usually a good reason why dogs bark, but some dogs do it so much and so loudly that owners and neighbours find it unacceptable. So the normal 'Who goes there?' territorial bark in response to, say, the postman might be tolerated, but not barking at passing birds or a falling leaf. It may be that your dog barks because he is stressed and lonely, a so-called separation behaviour, which we shall look at in more detail

'You would think that the punishment of a cold shower might stop them rolling in fox faeces. But it never does!'

There are numerous preparations on the market for removing or reducing the smell of dogs that have rolled in something unpleasant. There is a specific spray against skunk smell, which is probably the worst thing that can happen to a North American dog walker. For fox dung and other favourites, tomato ketchup rubbed over the affected area is said to be to be a useful preliminary to a full-scale shampoo wash. However, I won't pretend to understand the chemistry, and ketchup manufacturers seem reluctant to do the research and develop this particular application for their product!

in Chapter 6. Then again, many dogs bark in excitement, perhaps at the prospect of feeding or exercise. Finally, there are old dogs who sometimes bark as a form of self-stimulation, probably because they are deaf. Senile dementia afflicts many dogs and inappropriate or mistimed barking is a common complaint with owners of canine seniors (see Chapter 9).

There is no single management procedure that is relevant to all these categories and causes of barking, except that you may reap a life-long benefit from positively training your dog to bark on command (see page 94).

Case Study: **Monty the Guide Dog**

In a few severe cases where dung-rolling was so frequent as to threaten the dog's future, I have devised a training intervention. The owner of one such dog was blind and her guide dog Monty would roll in faeces during his out-of-harness free exercise. The behaviour threatened to destroy an otherwise good working relationship, so I had to act creatively. I equipped the owner with the remote-control spray collar Master Plus, where a hiss of gas is released by radio control at the moment the rolling begins. It is unpleasant for the dog, but effective because the context is unusual (a smelly stimulus), the timing is exact and of course it does not seem to be connected to the owner. In Monty's case, the owner's sighted partner operated the equipment and the outcome was positive, so he can continue to perform his duties as a guide dog.

Myth-Busting: Yes, It Helps to Train a Dog to Bark on Command

You may ask why on earth you would train a dog to bark, when what you really want in life is a quiet dog, or at worst one who only barks occasionally and at times you want. But that is precisely the purpose of this training exercise: to bring barking under your control, using the well-established principles of instrumental conditioning. This is what you do.

Wait for the dog to bark for whatever reason and give the command 'speak'. You might also give a signal such as a raised finger or making an O shape with your lips. Praise and reward the dog for each bark that is successfully linked to those signals. Pretty soon, he should have learned the association between his barking, your signals and a treat payoff. Once he gives a reliable response to your 'speak' command, introduce some extinction trials. From now on, whenever your dog spontaneously barks at times you would rather that he did not, penalize him by ignoring him. Before long he will find that the only barking that is rewarded is the formal, instructed response; in any other context it is so much wasted effort.

Everything in your dog's behaviour happens for a reason, and he barks because there is a payoff for him doing so. The most likely reward is that he will obtain more attention from you, even to the extent of your shouting and throwing things in his direction. At least the poor animal can rationalize that he is being noticed! So maybe a better strategy is to ignore him or apply a stimulus such as the Aboistop that will not

If barking is stimulated by birds or events outside the home, do something to prevent the dog seeing out of windows or through the garden fence.

inadvertently reward the unwanted response. Another possibility has come from observation of dogs wearing any design of head collar, such as the Halti or the Gentle Leader. Gentle pressure on the muzzle by these devices can exert a dramatic calming and quietening effect. The idea has been incorporated into a problem-solving accessory, the 'Quiet Dog', from Tellington Touch practitioner Susan Sharpe. It is constructed from soft elastic in a figure-of-eight form that is said to activate specific calming acupuncture points by exerting maintained pressure around the muzzle. Whatever the theory, it works!

If you have two or more dogs, it is possible that one barks to deliver a message to the other, who reciprocates. Pity the poor neighbours! Usually there is a ringleader who starts the barking and who should be closely monitored and if need be controlled with an Aboistop, a 'ssh' sound or Pet Corrector. This is the individual you should focus on with the 'bark on command' training described in the box above.

If yours is a quiet house where every little creak and rumble can be picked up, invest in noise, any kind of noise. One British talk radio

I have a friend Sandy who has accumulated
too many Border Terriers and I can hear her
coming from maybe a mile away! Her dogs
travel in the rear of a station wagon, but
behind a dog guard that prevents her from
even attempting to intervene. Sandy has an
out-of-control family of terrier terrorists!
The only solution would be for her to
deal with them one by one and somehow
to separate them when travelling. This is
practically impossible for her and she prefers
to turn up the radio, ignore the amusement
of others and just keep on driving.

Lots of 'bad' behaviour in dogs is only an attempt to gain
your attention. Isolating him from you and the rest of the
family until he is quiet is an effective learning strategy.

station, Radio 4, has apparently been used by
wildlife conservationists as a fox repellent, but to
me it just provides an intelligent window onto
the world. So it is good for you and comforting
for your dog to have background speech that
drowns out unusual sounds.

the same applies in the home if the dog is over-
excited by your preparing for the walk. And of
course phrases such as as 'let's go', 'walkies' or
'all dogs out', which cue your intentions, are best
outlawed if you want a peaceful life. Disciplined
travelling habits are best created from a young

'If yours is a quiet house where every little creak and rumble can be picked up, invest in noise, any noise'

The Bad Traveller: Dogs in Cars

I receive many calls for advice on how to deal
with dogs that behave badly in the car on the
journey to the park or forest, but rarely are there
complaints about the same dogs returning home.
We have all seen dogs in cars excitedly yapping,
jumping from side to side, with a harassed driver
struggling to maintain concentration and to be
safe on the road. The strategy for resolving these
in-car problems is to stop and not proceed until
and unless the dog is calm and quiet. Exactly

age, with a puppy held by a passenger on the
back seat. Take him with you on boring errands
to, say, the supermarket, where he will not be
released, so that he doesn't always associate the
car with having fun.

The reason dogs bark in cars is that they have
learned that it modifies our driving behaviour:
the more they bark, the faster we drive. At
journey's end, the more they bark, the quicker
we are to release them. Once the habit has been
formed, journeys from home to park provide the

cue for excited barking, whereas the homeward drive is subdued because home is boring.

Over the years, I have devised several methods to combat this, first and foremost being counter-conditioning so that barking in the car leads to a delay in departure. Just stay quietly at the wheel and wait until he stops. If it is safe to do so when he barks during the journey, again stop driving until he stops and proceed when he is quiet. When you arrive at your destination, don't rush to release him – make him wait. Maybe listen to the radio, get out and walk around the car and let the dog out only when he has been silent for, say, 30 seconds. Condition a 'sit' or 'down-stay' response prior to opening the car door. This

'The homeward drive is subdued because home is boring'

prevents the dog from running out before you have time to attach the lead.

For really serious cases of in-car hysteria, we find that bringing the dog forward into the rear passenger foot-well and behind the driver's seat reduces stimulation from the car's sideways movements. I advise tethering the dog so that his head is almost at ground level and he can't see the world outside. Ideally, have someone sit in the back seat to interact with him so that he gets more attention for being silent than noisy.

To Sum Up

As I said at the start of this chapter, nothing I have dealt with here deserves the description 'behavioural problem'. In the next chapter I will consider genuine problems where the penalty of failure is more painful for you, for your dog and for others.

The Car Is a Dangerous Place

This is true for dogs as well as for humans. The driver being distracted might lead to a collision or sudden braking, causing injury to a dog that is not restrained. I'll talk more about ensuring your dog's safety in Chapter 8 (page 156), but remember also that dogs die in cars during summer. The interior of a car – even in overcast Britain – can heat to more than 50°C (122°F) in less than ten minutes. Every year, in every country, we hear of tragic mistakes by careless owners, leading to horrible deaths for the dogs. If you must travel with the dog during hot weather, invest in air-conditioning, park in shade leaving windows open and always carry an emergency supply of water. These are such basic and obvious points that you would think they were not worth making. Unfortunately, even canine professionals who should know better have made these mistakes and killed their dogs.

If you are able to control your dog's behaviour, he will feel safe and cared for in new environments.

6 Canine Behavioural Therapy

Techniques for more serious issues

Canine Behavioural Therapy

The more serious behavioural problems in dogs, including fearfulness, fighting and phobias. Not to mention trying to dominate you and taking a dislike to your visitors. Don't worry – you can train your dog out of all these bad behaviours, either by yourself or with the help of a canine professional.

When I opened my 'animal psychiatry' practice in the late 1970s it was considered by the press to be a somewhat avant-garde indulgence for pampered pets. Since then, however, the notion that dogs may need specialist help to cope with the demands of modern living has come to be regarded as unremarkable and even useful, there now being a near army of individuals who ply for trade as 'behaviourists', 'whisperers' and the like. I liken our role to the humble status of 'fixers' of everyday problems in dogs, to be hired or fired as a plumber is judged by his ability to fix a leaking tap or a broken boiler.

I came to the field as a scientist with a background in the meticulous collection of data from observing dogs, cats and other animals in free-living and in laboratory situations. But within months of beginning the practice, I realized that lab-based research was a poor starting point from which to deal with the

'What was needed was a very particular approach, uniquely tailored to each and every dog'

Some canine behavioural problems are down to more than just a lack of training, but can be traced to abuse from an early owner or a traumatic experience.

variety and complexity of situations that confront domestic dogs. What was needed was a very particular approach for each and every dog, with therapeutic interventions or training programmes uniquely tailored to that individual.

So it is that, over the years, I have devised ways of dealing with many of the behavioural challenges that dogs present to their people. But even after all these years, I still see remarkable behaviours that do not get a mention in the professional literature. I was recently faced with a Bearded Collie who insisted on only turning left during walks around the streets of London. This was only the second such case I had encountered, and the other was also a Bearded Collie. Maybe they were related. I have also come across three Pugs which, in different households, would all frantically lick air around cigarette smoke. We found on close examination that this apparently odd behaviour was connected with the dogs' split palates, a common disorder in Pugs.

In this chapter, I will be describing the behavioural problems I treat most frequently. The list is by no means exhaustive, but much of it may help you to prevent such problems from developing in your pet, or to deal with them if they do. However, I should emphasize that the science of dog behaviour and the practice of dog training are constantly evolving and you the reader must pick and choose the bits that seem best to apply to your situation or that produce the best outcomes for your dog.

Seeking Professional Help

If you need help with your dog, first ask the advice of your veterinarian. You can't approach a specialist direct because a clinical examination is needed before embarking on any programme of behaviour modification or therapy. As with humans, many medical conditions impact upon canine behaviour, so your vet is an important partner in the dog-owner-trainer triangle.

Critically check out the claims, qualifications and experience of any canine professional before you commit money and the welfare of your pet to them. More important than academic qualifications are the practical, hands-on skills of dog management. Do they genuinely love the job, love dogs and want to help you make a success of your relationship with your dog?

During the first consultation, watch how the trainer interacts with your dog. Do they want to go out for walks or a short car ride, explore each and every aspect of your life with the dog, ask about how he behaves at the vet's, the groomer's, when you clip his nails, when left tethered? Do they focus on critical events that may have occurred in the past and especially during puppyhood? To do this job well, we canine professionals have to ask lots of questions and sometimes on subjects that might seem intrusive. There has to be a search for truth if we are to understand the likely causes and consequences of a behavioural problem.

Try to choose a canine professional who loves the job and has real empathy with his canine patients.

If you meet the mother when you are choosing a puppy, you will have a chance to observe her temperament and general state of health, in the hope that she will have passed good genes on to her offspring. Ideally see the father too.

Common Causes of Problems

Of course, much of what we are is encoded in our genes and there is a vast, ever-increasing output of scientific papers dealing with the subject of behavioural genetics. The genetic code for dogs, as for mice and men, has now been revealed and specific genes that regulate particular metabolic processes and target many behaviours have been identified. However, with the current state of knowledge, there seems little chance of gene therapy having much practical impact on how we treat behavioural problems in dogs. But if you are buying a puppy, it is sensible to go to a breeder whose dogs present desirable behavioural traits and avoid those that are nervous, aggressive or unresponsive to human contact. Whether these traits are inherited or acquired, it is certain that parent dogs markedly affect the behaviour and temperament of their offspring.

Fear

The major cause of excessive fearfulness in adult dogs is that they were not sufficiently stimulated and socialized during their first few months of life. I have dealt with this important topic in Chapter 2 (page 37), so suffice it to say here that both breeders and owners must invest time and effort into the rearing of puppies, because that will pay immense dividends when the puppy grows up.

Home Visit versus Specialist Centre

Most of the behaviour problems that occur in dogs are best dealt with in the home environment, where it matters and where a lot of unwanted behaviour occurs. However, there may be practical reasons why you have to go to a canine professional rather than him or her coming to you. If this is the case, it is important to present the behaviourist or trainer with a clear and honest account of the behaviour, when it began, how you believe it began, where and when it occurs and whom it mostly affects. If possible, supplement this information by filming examples of the problematic behaviour (the joy of having a smart phone). The behaviourist may then be able to come up with a theoretical analysis of the problem without seeing direct evidence of its consequences on your home and family.

Trauma

The most likely reason for a dog to be aggressive towards other dogs is that he himself has been the victim of an attack. It is a traumatic experience for any young dog, and very few such events are needed to turn a dog into a fighter. However, my practical experience is that dogs that have been the victim of attacks can be rehabilitated. Similarly, dogs that have been beaten and exposed to unimaginable cruelty also seem, in most cases, to make remarkably good recoveries and even continue to trust those who have abused them. Like many abused children, dogs are just too forgiving of the very people who cause them harm.

Clinical/Medical Causes

Just as our moods and emotions are affected by pain, hormonal and central nervous system disorders, so are those of our dogs. In this large family of medical causes, pain is the single most important trigger of unwanted behaviours. It may be a trapped nerve, arthritic joints or a host of other musculo-skeletal problems. Curiously, the most tangible and easily diagnosed sources of pain are untreated gum and dental disease and ear infections. Too many owners don't pay sufficient attention to the state of their pet's mouth or look to see what is going on in their ear canals. You may be in for an unpleasant surprise when you do!

Aggression: the Number One Complaint about Dog Behaviour!

Dogs are carnivores and carnivores kill. That is why dogs chase livestock, but it is generally not why they bite people: humans are not for eating! Rather, dogs bite people because (usually) they are afraid, feel threatened, there is competition over some resource, the home environment has been trespassed on or there is a dispute over leadership roles. The approach to

Myth-Busting: Tough Laws Don't Control Dangerous Dogs

The sad reality is that in almost every country monitored, reports of dog bites and of dogs attacking people are on the increase. Yet we have ever tougher laws intended to 'control' dangerous dogs, and there are ever-increasing numbers of canine behaviourists at work. Could there be some connection here? Perhaps tougher dog laws are not the solution to dealing with aggressive dogs, and some/many/most behaviourists just may have 'got it wrong'!

The way forward lies in better education of dogs, their owners and of course our wider society so that the needs and habits of dogs are better understood.

Using reward-based training while playing with a favourite toy is a great way to build a shy dog's confidence.

treatment greatly depends upon the underlying cause. Plainly a dog that is fearful of being approached, let alone touched, by strangers, requires very different management from one that is determined to be the top dog and objects to his people doing the things that people like to do.

The Fearful Dog

You can easily recognize the body language of a fearful dog: tail down and even tucked between his legs, dilated pupils, ears back and overall body shape showing conflict between approach (attack) and avoidance (retreat).

Plainly there needs to be a confidence-building programme here, but that same fearful dog has also been learning that a forward approach (ie. attack) can stop the unwelcome attention of humans. While gentleness and even a little pity may be appropriate, there also needs to be

a realistic assessment of the mislearning that has led to the development of this behaviour. However, you are more likely to make progress with such a dog using reward-based techniques. Accordingly clicker training (see page 70) would be my first choice for attempting to 'bring out' the personality of a fearful dog, even if it has bitten.

First of all, practise clicker training on other aspects of your dog's behaviour, using treats or whatever else motivates him. Play is a great motivator for many dogs, so choose games with a favourite toy to bring out his best. Then, when you are ready to deal with the fear issue, click or target each and every gesture where the dog comes forward to make (slightly) more confident contact with people, with dogs or whatever else he is afraid of. Be patient and encouraging at all stages.

'Play is a great motivator for dogs, so choose games with a favourite toy to bring out his best'

Counter-Conditioning or Response Substitution Training

Anxious or fearful dogs that retreat or, worse, defend themselves by biting an approaching human can be greatly helped if they are taught to engage in a behaviour or to adopt a posture

Myth-Busting: To Drug or Not to Drug?

Psychopharmacology is the general term for the use of drugs to modify behaviour. In human psychiatry, an array of compounds is used to change emotions and feelings. Many of these drugs have acquired bad reputations for their unwanted side effects: librium, valium (diazepam), ACP and many steroidal compounds have come and then gone out of fashion. Just the same trends seem to apply in the world of veterinary psychopharmacology. In the 1970s and '80s, it was common to treat aggressive dogs with megestrol acetate (trademarked Megace in the USA and Ovarid in the UK). Nowadays, nobody would dream of using this compound because of the effects it has on water retention, causing mammary tumours, making dogs fat and thus more liable to diabetes and yet more harmful side effects.

The trend of the world's drug manufacturers is to redirect their marketing efforts from humans to animals because they seem to represent a lucrative market for their products: pets are just like people, aren't they? Unfortunately, many of my veterinary colleagues across the globe have apparently been duped by flawed trials of this or that drug. Too often, the alternative, straightforward behavioural approach is not considered, and learned, usually normal adaptive behaviours such as a dog being upset when alone or attacking his owner are presented as though they were medical syndromes or abnormalities.

I have rarely found drug treatment necessary and when it has been, it was a last and even desperate resort. For instance, I acknowledge that the short-term use of medication can be helpful for the treatment of extreme and disabling fear of bangs or for the acute management of obsessive and self-destructive dogs, but in my practice, such cases arise only once or twice per year.

Fortunately there is a rising tide of consumer reaction against the over-prescription of psychoactive drugs, to people as well as to our pets. There are benign homeopathic and herbal alternatives that are as or more effective than drugs such as clomipramine and fluoxetine. One brand, Homeopet Anxiety, has been subjected to strictly controlled scientific testing in a study of dogs afraid of firework bangs. It was found to significantly reduce their fears compared to a control group given a placebo. The design of the experiment can greatly affect the outcome of these studies, and sadly the claims made for heavyweight veterinary prescription drugs are flawed because they performed no better in practice than the placebo. The same 'no better than chance' outcomes were found in the manufacturer-sponsored trials of the so-called pheromone products, which are also claimed to reduce fear in dogs. Caveat emptor!

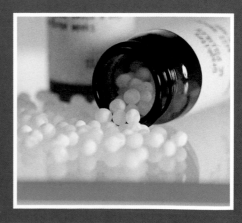

that prevents them from retreating or biting. The simplest option is 'sit'; or you could train him to 'go to his bed' or to sit on a mat within sight but out of reach of the visitor, if it is visitors that upset him. Alternatively, enjoyable trick training such as 'rolling over', 'playing dead' or 'lying on your side' might block his opportunities to engage in voluntary, fear-motivated behaviours. This counter-conditioning approach should be taught well ahead of the dog being exposed to the frightening stimulus, and should always be reward-based.

Another good way forward is to use a head collar and harness in combination, then oblige the dog to go for a walk either with you or with the person he seems to be afraid of. This requires both physical skills and confidence: he should certainly not be dragged on a choke chain nor even a conventional collar, and your confidence (or lack of it) will be readily transmitted to the anxious dog. Voice and total body language are crucial here. Take him forwards and towards objects and situations from which he wants to withdraw. However, the notion of systematic desensitization (a little at a time) should be your mantra: don't force him into an overwhelmingly frightening situation.

It is vital that you eliminate any possibility of your dog hurting someone. Fit a muzzle that allows him to pant, drink and even accept treats. A comfortably fitting muzzle eliminates any anxieties you may have that he will hurt you, members of your family or stooges you have recruited for the confidence-building programme.

If the dog does snap at you or your helpers, do not retreat or seem to provide him with the payoff of being left alone from unwanted contact. Hold your place, talk to him soothingly and, if possible, gently massage his ears.

Fake Fear

I am always mindful that some dogs make very convincing actors, presenting the body language of extreme fear when in reality their more truthful physiological signs are of a well-balanced or even confident dog. It is easy to condition or train these appearances of anxiety or timidity by responding to them with sympathy and support. The learning paradigm for the dog is simple: look scared, evoke pity from owner and the payoff is to be lavished with concerned attention! Children sometimes use the same ruse to manipulate their parents, and as a psychologist I again advise counter-conditioning to produce the opposite outcomes to those that the child (or dog) really wanted.

But appearances alone can be deceptive, and it can require considerable skill and technical support to differentiate fake fear from genuine distress. Look for a combination of symptoms such as dilated pupils (they dilate in the frightened dog), increased heart rate, changed muscle tone, hyperventilation, salivation and, for the technically minded, salivary cortisol levels. One or a combination of these signs should provide a reliable clue to the dog's true emotions.

If you conclude that your dog is not, after all, so distressed and is exaggerating his signs of fear in order to get more attention (the likeliest payoff), to be carried or taken home, for example, then institute the alternative strategy of cheerful 'jolly hockey sticks' and extrovert support.

'Tellington Touch' therapy see page 161 is now a well-established way of encouraging a nervous dog to respond to human contact. It is based on gentle massage of sensitive spots such as the ears.

'The payoff of engaging in extrovert activities must be greater than the penalty which comes from isolation'

The technique of ear massage is formalized in 'Tellington Touch' therapy (see Chapter 8), and you can usefully incorporate it into your pet-care regimes. A key part of 'TT' therapy is that the dog is lightly massaged on responsive parts of his body, and nowhere is more responsive in dogs (and perhaps people) than their ears. TT therapy nowadays has a worldwide network of practitioners who work to ethical standards and specialize in building up confidence in anxious dogs. Much of the theory behind TT derives from traditional Chinese medicine and specifically from acupuncture.

One very pragmatic way to harness the power of acupuncture principles for calming unwarranted fears in dogs is to use an Anxiety Wrap™. This is a close-fitting robe designed by an American TT practitioner and dog trainer, Susan Sharpe. It works by placing long-acting, mild pressure upon specific acupuncture points along the dog's body that are known to affect his emotions. It exerts an almost immediate effect of reducing fear, but without significant side effects except to make the dog look rather eccentric in a total-cover penguin suit! The Anxiety Wrap and another similar product, the Thundershirt,

have both been subject to independent and objective trial by the University of Tufts School of Veterinary Medicine in Massachusetts. They were found to be effective, with better results attributed to the Anxiety Wrap because it offers more sustained acupressure upon relevant points on the animal's body.

Overall, therapy for a fearful dog should be designed to provide positive payoffs for confident or extrovert activities and their linked emotions. The payoff of engaging in outgoing and extrovert activities must be greater than the penalty that comes from retreat and social isolation.

Noise Phobias: Fear of Bangs and Thunder

Dogs are unusual for developing extreme and disabling fears towards certain loud noises, primarily thunderstorms and explosive bangs from fireworks and gunfire. I am never called to treat noise phobias in cats, horses or any other species of domestic animal, and I don't know why dogs are so different in this respect. At least a quarter of dogs show an exaggerated fear of bangs and, depending on where you live, probably as many are oversensitive to storm systems. Thunderstorms are a rarity in the UK and so is the associated fear in dogs. However, in the Midwest of the USA and in central Europe, storms can be a daily occurrence during the summer and many dogs become extremely agitated as they approach. Indeed, an affected dog can seemingly predict the onset of a storm hours before people are aware of it, presumably because dogs are sensitive to the combined signs of increased humidity, temperature, time of day and changes in air pressure.

There is nothing so distressing as the sight of a dog pacing, panting and trying to escape from loud noises. They are aware of nothing else and are inconsolable in their fear, sometimes trying to escape the house and causing damage as they do so. Treating these irrational fears is one of the most challenging tasks we face in canine behavioural practice, but the key concept and tool for therapy is systematic desensitization. This is the psychological technique of offering a stimulus at an initially low and tolerated level, then gradually increasing the intensity or duration of exposure as the patient's tolerance improves, all the time pairing it with pleasant experiences or symbolic associations. That is how psychotherapists treat people who are afraid of snakes or spiders and it can also be applied to dogs that are afraid of noises, but with difficulty.

In Summary: Treatment of a Noise-phobic Dog

- Try systematic desensitization with relevant pre-recorded material.
- Provide a sound-proofed den to which he can escape.
- Keep him indoors and provide masking background music.
- Experiment with homeopathic or anxiety-relief medicines.
- Fit home-made or proprietary tight-fitting garments like the Anxiety Wrap.
- Judge whether or not to comfort or to distract the dog during episodes of extreme fear.

The challenge we face is to find sound recordings and playing equipment of sufficient quality to 'fool' the dog that this is the same stimulus as a real firework or thunder crack. It is very hard to produce a good version of reality from even the best recording. Nevertheless, you should try applying this technique to your dog using one of the many CD recordings that are sold for the purpose. I have prepared one such recording (in the Clix range), which covers all the principal

Wearing this face wrap calms anxious dogs but it is not a muzzle.

Choose a design of muzzle that enables him to be patted, drink and even accept a treat while he is wearing it.

Training tricks such as 'rolling over' will help a dog realize that close contact with you is fun and stretches their considerable intelligence.

noises of which dogs are afraid. Start at a low volume on your best HiFi equipment and don't turn it up until your dog is seen to be relaxed at that intensity. Don't hurry this process and, if the dog seems distressed, reduce the volume again.

I have experimented with many other adjunctive therapies to treat severely sound-phobic dogs and have not found any merit in the many drugs that are specifically marketed to treat this problem. However, the homeopathic medicine Anxiety, mentioned earlier, has helped many of my patients to cope in the short term. Another widely used remedy is Bach Flowers, and there are also some proprietary herbal preparations recommended for phobias. There is anecdotal evidence that these treatments can be effective in some cases, but unfortunately most do not live up to their manufacturers' promise. The best line of treatment for storm- and bang-phobic dogs is a tight-fitting garment such as the American products Anxiety Wrap™ and Thundershirt™, mentioned earlier. The most important resource for a dog terrified by noise

is somewhere to escape, ideally a darkened inner den where he can dig into soft material and feel safe. In practice, this will usually be a crate to which he has been familiarized from puppy days, covered in duvets or other sound-absorbing material. Play loud, distracting music while the offending noises rage outside and close windows, doors and curtains.

Your dog's awareness of sounds can also be reduced by fitting him with the same ear defenders that people use to protect their hearing in noisy environments. Acceptance of the specifically designed foam earplugs varies enormously from one dog to another and if your dog accepts them at all he will usually have to wear an elasticated bandage over his head so that he can't dislodge them. Your first attempt to install a foam hearing defender should be overseen by a vet to ensure that it is lodged in the correct part of the ear and can be removed without causing harm. Whether or not to acknowledge and comfort your dog when he is afraid is a very personal matter. For some dogs,

Thie Jack Russell hates his neighbour – me! I am making initial contact with a tidbit, then later we will walk together.

In Summary: Treatment of a Fearful Dog

- Prevention is better than cure. Invest in environmental and social enrichment of puppies and attend puppy classes.
- Identify and reward outgoing or extrovert behaviour.
- Use reward-based clicker training to develop new activities and postures that are incompatible with fearful withdrawal (counter-conditioning).
- Determine whether your dog really is as fearful as his body language suggests.

- If he is a fake (and many are), use a head collar and harness to lead him confidently and firmly towards the stimulus or person he wants to avoid.
- Get him used to being with other people: pass the lead and treats to strangers and have them build up even short-term relationships with your dog.
- Don't take risks of your dog biting, even in self-defence. Use a muzzle if there is that risk.

excessive displays of concern by the owner will worsen the external indications of anxiety in the dog ('fake fear'), but other dogs seem genuinely to be helped to cope by being cuddled and 'protected'. You must use your judgement on this issue and do what seems to work best with your pet. Relief from disabling fear of loud noises does eventually come to dogs when they become deaf and I have seen that process happen in my own little terrier PC. A worthwhile bonus for living to an old age.

Your Dog Bites Visitors: Territorial Defence

We all take pride in the possibility that our dog might defend us and our home against a burglar. Though be warned: the law in most European countries tends to favour the rights of the burglar over those of the householder. American attitudes are somewhat different, with a dog constituting a legitimate way to defend your home against those who might wish you harm.

The protective role of dogs was, for sure, one of the key drivers behind their original domestication. Their acute hearing and sense of smell alert us to intruders and most dogs can pack a mean bite. The trouble is, a dog that defends its territory against genuine foes may also bite those who have a legitimate reason to visit your home, such as family, friends or the postman. All in all, it is best not to encourage your dog to bite anyone, under any circumstances. Instead, you need to undermine the complex hierarchy of behaviours associated with a home-guarding dog – and, if needs be, make it you and not him who takes responsibility for defending it.

There are two key things to do if you want your dog to be sociable and trusting of people. First, select a breed known to be less territorial or suspicious of intruders than others; and second, actively socialize your dog so that he meets a wide variety of people early on in life and experiences positive outcomes from those encounters (see Chapter 2).

A conundrum that often arises here is that the dog may be generally tolerant of visitors but hate a specific type of person – say people in uniform or men with beards, anyone wearing motorcycle helmets or a turban, black people, white people

1 Chasing bicycles is another of those dangerous habits that your dog may exhibit if he has not been exposed to them from an early age. 2 Encourage a cyclist friend to stop, talk and give the dog time to investigate this unfamiliar machine. 3 Ask the cyclist to reward your dog's tolerance with a treat.

and so on. Such prejudices do not necessarily arise because dogs have been encouraged to be racist; it is rather that in early days they were not exposed to these categories of humankind. That is another key reason why you should be out and about with your puppy and attend classes in which a variety of people participate.

I have made many memorable house visits to treat overprotective, territorial dogs. It is a problem which does not 'travel' to a clinic, because by definition it is usually only seen close to home. So we have to demonstrate the appropriate training techniques in the home, where it matters.

The starting point is to train the dog to sit and stay in a particular location, perhaps on a mat in the hallway from which he can see visitors coming through the entrance door, without leaving his 'safe' spot on the mat. Pre-train the 'go to your mat' command and the 'sit' and 'stay' responses. During the early stages of this training it may be safest to tether the dog to a hook on the wall or to some heavy item of furniture.

Barking is often a key component in a spiral of behaviours that ultimately lead to the dog biting the visitor. So if we inhibit barking, we can also block him from going on to bite. Refer to Chapter 5 for the various techniques to stop barking, but in this instance I recommend trying an automated spray collar, which dissociates the penalty for barking from the presence of you or indeed of the visitor.

The third important way to reduce territorial behaviours is to create positive outcomes and expectations from contact with strangers or visitors to the home. The Swedish dog psychologist Anders Hallgren taught me this simple technique, which most trainers and behaviourists would now apply to such cases. Place a pot of treats at the front door with a note requesting visitors to take some and throw them in your dog's direction. Later, you might ask them to hand-feed the dog, once this can be done safely. The important thing for the dog is that he associates the visitor rather than you, the owner, with the treat payoff for adopting the sit-stay on the mat, near to the door.

The temptation to hold, restrain and 'comfort' a dog that is threatening to savage a visitor is often quite compelling. You don't want your dog

1 If your dog is agressive towards visitors, start by training him to 'sit' and 'stay'on a mat in the hall from which he can see anyone who comes in the door. 2 Keep a supply of treats handy and ask visitors to reward the dog. 3 When you are confident that this can be done safely, get visitors to hand-feed the treats. Your dog will soon learn that being friendly to visitors brings him lots of positive payoffs.

to hurt anybody, so you hang on to his collar and lead him to a back room of the house, away from trouble. Nothing could be more likely to train a threatening response to your next visitor. First, the dog is rewarded by your making physical and verbal contact in response to his barking

> 'If he can have one over on you, if he can get away with it, if you choose the 'wrong' moment to confront him, he will react badly'

and growling. Then, it is the presence of the visitor that precipitates the penalty of him being expelled away from your company. This is a very powerful scenario from which to condition territorial, aggressive behaviour.

Dominant Dogs: He May Bite You!

Most reported dog bites occur within the home and affect family members. How can it be that your best friend could bite your hand, the very hand that feeds him? The answer is rooted in the connection between social hierarchies and the payoffs he obtains by engaging in threatening as opposed to appeasing behaviour with people. Simply put, if he can have one over you, if he can get away with it, you choose the 'wrong' issue or the wrong moment to confront him, he will react badly and may even bite you. This is not a display of domestic violence but rather a natural, biological process because you have failed to develop consistent and kind rules that put you in charge, as opposed to the dog being in charge of you. As one British behaviourist, Colin Tennant, says, 'If you treat your dog like a human he will treat you like a dog!'

I have already explored the notion of social hierarchies in the world of dogs (see Chapter 3), but practically speaking there are some straightforward techniques to help you create winning ways in the leadership stakes.

Do not be in too much of a hurry to reverse long-established dominance disputes and never use violence. Remember that not all dogs who bite their owner do so out of a sense of dominance: there may be other reasons such as his being frightened or in pain. You may be pushing him too far when clipping his toenails or restraining him to treat an injury. Even in those cases, an investment in fair but consistent management should provide you with the authority needed to manage an unpleasant

In Summary: Making Your Dog Friendlier Towards Visitors

- Teach puppies social skills: these will last all their lives.
- If there is any possibility of your dog hurting anybody, fit a muzzle.
- Counter-condition a 'sit-stay' near the entrance to your home, where he can see but not touch the visitor. Tether him if necessary.
- Have visitors provide rewards (treats).
- Do not unintentionally reward the very

behaviour of which you disapprove. Change the payoffs and penalties in favour of friendly and less threatening behaviours.
- Maintain your dog's social skills by routinely walking him among and towards people, engaging them where possible to indulge and generally make friends with him.

A close-fitting 'anxiety wrap' such as this, makes dogs feel snug and less anxious.

Touch and physical contact are what dogs like, and Bounce likes it rough.

but necessary procedure. To achieve a leadership role over a dog (perhaps as over people), you do not need to be a despot, but rather someone who is calm, consistent and not easily subject to manipulation. We have all seen how clever dogs are at winkling that last uneaten crumb off your plate, at getting you out of bed in the morning by whining, at refusing to return on a

technique that has been advocated by a certain TV pundit, nor to string dogs up on choke chains until they seemingly submit. Such cruelty can only undermine your dog's trust in humanity and may lead to you and others being bitten.

Here instead is the Mugford Method for putting you back in control of your dog.

'You do not need to be a despot, but rather someone who is calm, consistent and not easily subject to manipulation'

recall because it is more fun to chase squirrels or have you retrieve the ball. These are all small but significant indications that your dog is playing games with you. Not good!

The rules for dominance management in dogs are well understood both by scientists and by behavioural practitioners such as myself. However, only some of what follows will be relevant to your situation, and if you have a problem with a dog who threatens or bites you, you should consult a canine professional. I certainly do not advise you to engage in physically rough and confrontational activities such as the so-called 'dominance rollover'

'Nothing in Life Comes Free'

Make sure that everything the dog wants, be it food, fun, walks or contact with other dogs, is earned by at least a sit-stay, and that these key resources come at times and places of your choosing, not of his.

Be careful not to inadvertently reward those unwanted, manipulative behaviours that dogs are so clever and persistent at performing. For instance, if he creates a commotion at the door or near where his lead is hanging, you can safely assume that he wants you to go for walkies. Don't give in! Rather, time the walk to coincide with his being quiet, calm and perhaps obeying a sit-stay

Nothing should come for free, so at least demand a 'sit' response before feeding your dog.

for a defined period. Don't let him assume that food is a 'given'. Again, he should 'work' for it. If needs be, feed him several small meals a day so that each provides a learning opportunity to show who is in ultimate control of this key resource.

If you give a command, feel obliged to enforce it. If you cannot (perhaps because he's running wild in the countryside and is too far away), stay silent. Wait until you are in a position to

somehow enforce that command to 'come'. An outdoor long-line or indoor houseline can be a crucial accessory to put you in charge of what might otherwise be a dog under his own control.

Elevation from the ground and access to comfortable spots like your sofa or bed confer a massive privilege to dogs. It is natural (and to me rather nice) that dogs want to lie with or even on us, but it is a privilege to be managed and not a right. Always exercise your prerogative to say 'no' or 'off'.

It is very important to apply consistent rules. One might be that a dog does not push past you in doorways or along corridors, but rather that he has to follow. Another might be that he must, from time to time, give up his favourite toy or chew.

Your tone of voice when giving a command can be really important. There is a widespread belief that men make better dog managers and trainers than women. I don't believe this, but on the rare occasions when it does seem to be the case, I find that it is very often a matter of voice. Women's voices are of a higher frequency and are less likely to have the scary, strained-intensity modulation of men. Of course there are

1 A puppy who has not learnt to share, perhaps because he was separated from his siblings at an early age, may be possessive of his toys. 2 Use substitution techniques to encourage him to let go. Be gentle and patient at all times, but make it clear who is in charge. 3 Reward him with a treat when he releases his toy.

exceptions, but a good shout can come in handy when a dog is seriously out of order.

Finally, the manner in which obedience training is conducted is important. Choose trainers and training classes that take a balanced approach. Emphasize the need to reward positive outcomes but retain the option of applying well-timed penalties when the dog chooses his way rather than yours.

Fighting: Dog-to-Dog Aggression

It is natural for dogs to fight, because that is the way they compete for resources such as space, food and mates. In fact, it is remarkable that most dogs are for most of the time peaceful creatures who positively enjoy each other's company. But a few do not: they would rather fight other dogs or, at best, will fight back when they feel threatened. This is a normal biological process that in former times would probably never have been regarded as a 'behavioural problem'. But a problem it is, because both

Castration!

Seven out of ten dog bites in the home are by males, and most by entire males. Castration makes dog management less stressful and more benign. A castrated dog need not be a boring dog and the removal of testosterone can have a wide range of beneficial consequences for canine behaviour.

dogs and people who mistakenly intervene in a fight are likely to be hurt. In my experience, the commonest reason that dog owners in Britain are prosecuted for having a dog which is 'dangerously out of control' and causes an injury is that someone unwisely intervened to break up a dog fight.

Males are much more likely to fight than bitches, which suggests that there is a strong endocrine component to the behaviour. A dog

'It is remarkable that most dogs are for most of the time peaceful creatures who enjoy each other's company'

In Summary: Preventing Your Dog from Dominating You

- Make it clear at all times that it is you who are in charge. Make him 'work' for food, walks and treats.
- Don't give a command that you can't enforce.
- Consider castrating an over-assertive male dog.
- Be firm and be consistent. Combine payoffs and penalties to achieve the behaviours you want.

can discriminate the hormonal state and in all likelihood the social status of another dog by the chemicals in his urine, on his breath and in sebaceous glands on the body. So castration – which reduces the levels of testosterone and other hormones he produces – not only reduces the motivation to pick fights, but it also greatly reduces the likelihood of his being attacked by other males.

Dogs learn social skills with other dogs through play, which again emphasizes the importance of early socialization among a wide variety of dog sizes, types and ages. Play is the best mediator and even if it sometimes seems to be somewhat violent, it is highly therapeutic and

Old dogs allow puppy pestering that they would not tolerate from an adult.

source of mild interest to village folk. Usually the dogs were left to sort out their differences in a dominance-determining dispute. Just occasionally, someone might throw a bucket of water over them, but not once can I recall dogs being seriously injured or killed in such fights. It is still much the same throughout less developed or rural parts of Asia, Africa or South America: given the freedom to roam and to socialize, dogs maintain their social skills and do not engage in mortal combat.

Matters are just a bit different now when, in almost every developed country and in almost every place, dogs have to be under control on a leash. This denies them opportunities to make unrestricted contact with other dogs and has produced a marked deterioration in their social skills, the improvement of which is the primary objective behind the programme of therapeutic retraining that follows.

dogs should generally be left to their own devices.

But what if your dog makes that crucial transition from competitive play to violent, damaging fighting? I was raised on a farm where there were many dogs that came from the nearby village. It was safe for them to roam and dog fights would, from time to time, be a

Competition between dogs for a favourite toy or bone, is one indication of relative social hierarchy. Changing or disputed social ranks can be violent and people had best stay away.

What to Do

First make a checklist of the dogs that your dog does not like. Are they differentiated by sex, by size, even by colour? Very often it is dogs of a particular type, say boxers with their square faces, black Labradors, very large or very small dogs that are the target. Plainly it is not the fault of these victim dogs to be of their specific breed or physiognomy, but it as well to be prepared for trouble. Invest in a muzzle and a long-line, so that you can manage your dog while he is at a distance from you and you can walk towards other dogs, confident that you can still safely intervene to interrupt a fight.

Your body language, what you say and what you do are crucial as your dog approaches other dogs. In all likelihood, he is using you as the rationale for initiating a fight – you are the most

> 'Your body language, what you say and what you do are crucial as your dog approaches other dogs'

important resource in his world and the closer he is to you and the shorter his lead is, the more he sees the other dog as something to be driven away.

To overcome this problem you will need the assistance of other dog owners. It is unfair to just pitch in to any dog you find in the park, because every threat or potential injury can have a contagious effect: your carelessness could turn that dog victim into yet another socially insecure fighter of other dogs.

Keep Your Distance

With a well-briefed friend or dog trainer acting as a stooge, test how close your dog can be to the other before he becomes aroused. The obvious signs are raised hackles, tail up, continuous threatening eye contact, then a growl before launching an attack. If it gets to that stage, you have misjudged the situation and have brought your dog too close to the stooge.

Work on the distance within which your dog remains relaxed rather than becoming antagonistic. It may be as much as 100m (100 yards or so), or it may be much closer. Does your dog provide clear and honest signals of his intentions, or are they corrupted? In some breeds (for instance in true Pit Bull Terriers) there has been a selection in favour of inhibited or corrupted body signals where the intention to launch an attack has been subverted in favour of a stealthy, non-threatening demeanour, followed by a sudden onslaught. This phenomenon is sometimes described in popular canine literature as 'predatory drift', with dogs (and it is often Bull breeds) suddenly switching from passive or playful interactions with other dogs to a seemingly unprovoked attack. However, the term 'predatory drift' does not have any serious scientific credentials and no dog that I know actively predates upon other dogs with a view to eating them!

Management of the distance between you and the opponent or stooge dog is a crucial part of

Meta communication or exhange of dogs' signals between these two friends is too fast for a human to follow.

Safe and total control must be the first priority when training an aggressive dog as here with Charli on a Halti and double-ended lead.

In Summary: Preventing Dog Fights

- Keep your potentially aggressive dog muzzled and on a long lead, so that he can wander away from you while still being under your control.
- Practise with a well-informed friend or canine professional, rather than letting your dog loose with strangers in the park.
- Gradually bring him closer to you and reward him for not being aggressive when other dogs approach.
- Use a head collar and harness so that you can turn an aggressive forward lunge into a vulnerable side-on position.
- Payoffs and penalties: carry a Pet Corrector just in case things go wrong, but also have a supply of treats to reward each success and to enable you to make friends with other dogs.

the training process. Too close, too fast and you cannot deliver the rewards or signs of approval for his tolerance. Reward in such situations is more beneficial than having to intervene dramatically and punish your dog for a display of aggression.

Stopping a Fight

There may, however, be moments when matters do get out of hand, the best laid plans go wrong and you have a near or actual dog fight on your hands. This is when you might feel the need to interrupt the combatants.

My preferred aid is the hiss sound from a Pet Corrector aerosol (see page 89). However, subtle management of the direction of your dog's face and body can also provide a useful penalty to discourage fights. The Halti head collar allows the trainer to steer a dog's gaze to the side, so that he can't pull forward. However, the same process also enables a would-be fighter to present the vulnerable side of his face and his body to the opponent dog. The Halti can be combined with a harness, enabling you to manipulate the dog's complete head and body so that, instead of a forward lunge, he ends up in an embarrassing sideways-on position. This is a crucial skill that you might benefit from working on with a canine professional and an unflappable trained stooge dog with which to practise the technique.

Success!

The ultimate goal is for your dog to be allowed off lead in the company of other dogs. As you progress from tight regulation near other dogs, you might drop the long-line so that it trails behind him, while he is muzzled. Let him approach and have relatively free contact with others, but stay close enough to grab the lead if there is any prospect of his launching an attack.

As the frequency of threats diminishes and you estimate that the risk of fights is negligible, there may come a time when you can consider removing the long-line altogether, then later removing the muzzle too. However, I must emphasize that this is a very big step indeed, and you must ensure that your dog is genuinely a reformed character who is safe and sociable in the company of other dogs. A radio-controlled spray collar may enable the necessary long-distance control that is needed to responsibly manage the risks of another fight.

Curbing the Hunter: Livestock Chasing

What could be more natural than that dogs should hunt? In a dog's mind, hunting is all about putting food on the table and enjoying the fun of the chase, so shouldn't really be considered to be part of the aggression complex. However, the penalties for dogs that chase and kill farm animals can be severe. In the UK, the law allows a farmer to shoot a dog that he catches in the act of chasing his livestock. Sheep are the species most likely to be targeted by city and suburban dogs. However, in a survey I conducted in a rural part of the UK, it was bored farm collies that were overwhelmingly involved

in fatal attacks upon sheep. The retraining of dogs who chase livestock has provoked animated argument between those who believe that all dog training can be achieved by consistent and skilful use of rewards, versus those (like me) who see it as a perfect case for applying carefully

> ## 'Instead of a forward lunge, he ends up in an embarrassing sideways-on position'

timed punishment and subsequent reward for compliance. In my view, there has to be a penalty for engaging in this most natural of behaviours and a payoff for restoring the alternative. Fortunately, it is relatively easy to train a dog not to chase livestock and even easier to stop puppies gaining the habit. As ever, prevention is so much better than cure.

At my farm we have a selection of much-loved hand-reared sheep that have grown up among dogs and show no fear of them. Two ewes in

Cows have the advantage of size, intimidating a would-be potential herding puppy such as Buttons.

Curiosity among puppies is understandable when it comes to unfamiliar animals. A long-line is advisable.

particular, Horny and Fluffy, seem positively to enjoy the opportunity to pursue and punish would-be sheep chasers. I love to take parties of puppies among my sheep, who swarm towards the dogs knowing that there will be food hand-outs and that if puppies get in the way, they can be knocked aside. Meanwhile, the puppies learn that sheep do not always run away but rather are big, smelly and sometimes scary creatures that are best avoided.

When a puppy does begin to chase, I throw a rattly object such as a can of pebbles (see Chapter 3 for more about rattle-can training). If the timing is right, the effect can be remarkable. It is also a good example of one-trial learning in action, a phenomenon where a single significant penalty can change the behaviour of an animal for good. It works in much the same way as we learned as children not to touch hot stoves because of the one-trial (penalty) of experiencing a painful burn.

If you do not have access to tame sheep such as I have described, then the onus is on you as a responsible dog owner to avoid areas where vulnerable livestock are kept.

The key to treating a hardened livestock chaser is that there be a penalty that is ascribed to the target prey species (whether it be sheep, poultry, cattle, horses or wildlife), but not to the trainer or the owner. There are many in the world of dog training who would use an electric shock collar in such circumstances, but in my view this extremely aversive approach is not justified. A good high-tech but more humane alternative is to be found in radio-controlled spray collars (see Chapter 3).

My technique is to walk through pet sheep or close to tame chickens with a dog on a slack long-line. Have the spray collar (the penalty) at the ready and zap your dog at the moment he rushes towards or is close to the livestock (say within a metre/yard). He should, hopefully, be

In Summary: To Stop a Dog Chasing Livestock

- If possible, expose either a puppy or an adult dog to sheep or other livestock that are not frightened of him – he will learn to be wary of them.
- Devise appropriate penalties such as a rattle can or radio-controlled spray collar.
- If all else fails, avoid areas where you are likely to meet livestock, or keep your dog under close control.

The well-timed dropped can technique is a perfect penalty to interrupt the puppy who chases chickens

surprised and even a little distressed, so call him back to you and reward, praise and comfort him. Offer him treats for obeying the recall. Repeat, repeat and repeat. My experience is that if the timing is correctly handled, no more than three such exposures will produce a long-lasting aversion to that particular species.

Very often, however, aversion to livestock is specific to the particular context and the place where the training was conducted. It is likely, therefore, that exposures will have to be repeated at other locations, by other trainers and using a variety of species to be avoided. Otherwise, the animal will consider that livestock is dangerous and to be avoided only at location X, but not at Y and Z.

Over-Attachment

Of all the dogs I see in my practice, second only to those that bite, fight or kill are those that are over-attached and love their owners too much. Again, this is a natural phenomenon that we cultivate but then come to regret. What can be better than a dog that adores us, watches our every move and is always on hand to receive and return affection?

Unfortunately, their very devotion can lead to major problems when you and your dog have to be separated. The symptoms can be various,

such as the dog being destructive when left alone, howling, urinating or simply looking distressed and lonely. However, the underlying cause and the approach to treatment are the same for all these seemingly dissimilar symptoms.

The process whereby dogs become attached to people is well understood and is much the same in puppies as in human infants with their mothers. We tend to find puppies so adorable that we can barely put them down. We have to cuddle and indulge them, rewarding their every show of affection, dependence and vulnerability. This is the time when we create the fundamentals of the adult dog relationship with us and, importantly, their likely eventual response to separation. The management and metering of your love for a puppy is something to be disciplined about. Puppies soon learn how to manipulate us, so be on your guard against their

'What can be better than a dog that adores us and is always on hand to receive and return affection?'

A dog who is over-attached to his owners suffers emotional stress when left alone …

… destructive chewing and scratching are only symptoms of that distress.

Myth-Busting: When Puppy First Comes Home: Leave Him to Cry All Night or Take Him to Bed?

This is a dilemma that has to be faced when we bring puppy home from the breeder, where he probably had the company of siblings and mother at all times. Suddenly he is alone, deserted downstairs while his humans have gone away without leaving the familiar and comforting sounds and smells of his previous life.

I have no doubt that for the young puppy typically purchased at between 7 and 12 weeks, being left alone is a traumatic experience. It is nearly impossible to manage a training programme so that puppies get used to being isolated at such a young age, so I recommend that new puppy parents do take him to their bedroom for the first few weeks. Invest in a crate that can be placed alongside your bed, so that he has a compromise near-contact with you. Just as with a newborn baby, whom we would not dream of leaving alone to cry all night without being comforted, so it should be with a puppy. My experience is that the 'tough it out, turn over and let him cry' approach is not the best way to produce a long-term, trusting and confident relationship between a puppy and his new owners.

By 15 weeks, your puppy is maturing and you can gradually move him out of the bedroom (if that is what you would like) to the hallway, down the stairs and eventually to the kitchen, dog room or other place away from sleeping humans. But do it gradually and in an orderly and systematic fashion, so that the puppy learns that his world does not come to an end when he is away from human contact.

For his first weeks in your home, a puppy is likely to be much happier sleeping near you.

displays of distress or cute demands and resolve to assume control from the start. In particular, get your puppy used to being alone for brief periods, but see the box above.

In later adolescent and adult life, the same process of gradual separation from humans is the way forward. I see so many over-attached dogs who are allowed to follow and to be with people all the time, until the family go out and the dog is left alone.

If you have complaints from neighbours about your dog howling when you are out or perhaps find that the paintwork in your house is being systematically stripped by your dog in his attempts to rejoin you, then I suggest you apply the following desensitization programme.

If you return home and discover damage or hear of complaints about your pet barking, never scold or punish him. Any penalty you apply will be misconstrued because it will be given long after the unwanted behaviour occurred.

Your dog is in a state of fear, sometimes of near terror. Before leaving him alone, treat him as I earlier suggested you treat the fearful dog (see page 104), including use of the Anxiety Wrap and any other treatments you have found calm him down. Try reducing lighting levels by drawing curtains or administer proven herbal and homeopathic preparations.

Whereas you should be pleasantly affectionate in your greetings to the dog after he has been left alone, you should be cold or off-hand at the moment of your leaving. Too many of us are over-affectionate to our dogs prior to going out, making them feel all the more abandoned. Cold departures but warm returns are in order.

When you go out, try to leave behind physical,

the shops. Leave the house by different routes – even by the windows if that is what is needed to keep the dog guessing!

Don't park the car outside the house; sometimes leave it round the corner where it can't be heard. Don't always rattle house and car keys or go through the same exit routine of setting burglar alarms and so on.

If you have to leave your dog alone for any length of time and no one is coming in during your absence, wear him out. Spend time, perhaps

'If possible, leave home in work clothes on some occasions but wearing casual clothes on others'

chemical or auditory links to remind him that you are still connected. Leave the radio or TV on, or give him some unwashed items of clothing on which he can lie and maybe dream of you!

Owners who have to adhere to a predictable routine always find managing separation problems in their dogs more difficult. In an ideal world, your dog should not know for sure whether you will be out of the house for minutes or hours. If possible, leave home in work clothes on some occasions but wearing casual clothes on others as though you were just popping out to

an hour or more, sharing in exhausting and exciting experiences outdoors.

Food-dispensing toys are sometimes helpful if you have a dog that will work or is distracted by food. They are ideal for Labradors, for whom the hunger drive may be even bigger than their longing for human company. The first such device to be available commercially was the Buster Cube, but now there are many others that require a dog to invest time and effort in dislodging treats. But beware, most are noisy, so if you live in an apartment, it could annoy your

When you leave your dog alone, make sure that he has a favourite food-stuffed toy to occupy him during your absence.

A 'piddle pad' can be a helpful accessory when you are house-training your puppy. 1 Encourage your puppy to sniff and investigate.

2 Treat and reward for urinating on the mat. It is also useful for apartment-dwellers who find it difficult to take their dog outside every time he needs to 'go'.

neighbours. I'll look at alternatives to leaving your dog home alone in Chapter 8, but whatever you decide to do, it is really important not to consider an attachment problem a 'syndrome' or an abnormality. There is a fashion in veterinary literature to describe these behaviours as being a 'hyper-attachment syndrome', whereas nothing could be further from the truth. Insecure dogs are just animals that have chosen to love humans too much and perhaps more than we deserve.

Toileting Problems

Persistent house-soiling can create nightmare scenarios for owners because none of us want to face the hygiene issues it creates. There is the expense of replacing carpets, the constant

cleaning of floors and embarrassing moments when visitors comment on the smell....

There are some remarkable national differences in procedures and attitudes towards this problem. In Japan and many other Asian countries, the tendency is to keep dogs indoors or in a yard for most of the time and to train them to urinate or defecate at a particular location or in a special toilet zone. By contrast, most Europeans and North Americans expect their dog to 'go' outdoors, in the yard, in the garden or on walks.

Fortunately, the selection and even the timing of where and when dogs urinate and defecate is highly susceptible to payoffs (but less so to penalties). Puppies are greatly influenced by where their mother toilets and tend to follow her and then to 'go' close to where she has 'performed'. When you bring a puppy home, he is unlikely to follow you in the same way, but you can at least guide him towards selection of a particular place or a particular surface or substrate. Manufactured 'piddle pads' are popular with North American dog owners; in the UK and other European countries it is more common to train puppies to 'go' outside.

What matters is consistency, always being on hand to interrupt the puppy just before he chooses to urinate or defecate on the 'wrong'

In Summary: Toilet Training

- Train your puppy to 'go' in the same place, whether in the garden or yard, or in a pre-determined toilet zone.
- Feed in the morning to encourage defecation during the day rather than at night.
- Consider castrating a persistent indoor 'urine-marker'.

spot and then taking him to the 'right' place, be it indoors or out. After that, train the act of elimination to a simple word command such as 'go', 'busy' or the name of a not-so-popular relative. The same technique applies to both urination and defecation.

Many owners want to direct their dog to defecate at a particular time and at a particular place. This might be unrealistic because, as for us humans, so much depends upon when we

'An early-rising routine should reduce the risk of an overnight "accident"'

eat, what we eat and how physically active we are. However, dogs, like people, tend to defecate in the morning, so an early-rising routine should reduce the risk of an overnight 'accident'. Early-morning feeding will generally precipitate daytime defecation, whereas late-night feeding will provoke drinking and is more likely to produce overnight incontinence.

The matter of diet is also very important. I will deal with that in detail in the next chapter, but for the moment you need to be aware that, generally speaking, high-fibre diets are good for

dogs. However, they also increase the volume and frequency of defecation. Find a diet that provides the right compromise between firm stools and an acceptable volume and frequency of defecation. It is a matter for pragmatic experimentation.

Finally, owners of entire male dogs may have a problem with indoor 'marking', with the dog usually depositing small quantities of urine against vertical surfaces or the corners of furniture. This is particularly common in small dogs, especially when they visit someone else's house. Castration should put an end to this, but thereafter it is very important that the scent of previous urine marks be scrupulously removed with appropriate cleaning agents (see page 88).

Coprophagia

This is the technical term for the eating of faeces; it is a common complaint that owners make about their dogs and is especially prevalent in those that are kennelled or institutionalized. Numerous scientific studies have failed to produce any clear explanation for this behaviour: the most likely reason is that the dog is hungry and is taking on additional calories from the (relatively) high fat content of dog faeces.

The best approach to this problem is to feed your dog a diet that makes him feel satiated. Generally speaking, this means a high-fibre diet. Read the small print on dry foods, which usually have a higher fibre content than tinned or raw meat. However, the fibre content of commercial diets differs enormously from one brand to another; if your dog's favourite isn't very high in fibre, enhance it by adding green vegetables or scalded bran.

An alternative approach that sometimes has worked with my coprophagic patients has simply been to switch them to the Raw Meaty Bones or BARF regime that is described in the next chapter.

In Summary: Stop Your Dog Eating Faeces

- Feed him a high-fibre diet to make him feel full, and experiment with foods from a variety of manufacturers – home-cooked and raw.
- Use a radio-controlled spray training device to discourage opportunist coprophagia.

It may be that your dog is an opportunistic eater of other dogs' faeces (or, in urban parks, leftovers of discarded fast foods) when out on walks, but does not eat his own. This problem justifies the use of a penalty in the form of a radio-controlled spray-training device, such as the French-manufactured Master Plus. As always, good timing is essential; it is also important that you remain silent and do not seem to be the source of the remotely delivered penalty.

Don't Despair If Yours Is a Problem Dog!

In this chapter I have taken you through the most common and serious behavioural problems that clients bring to me and to other professionals like me. You probably feel pretty good that your dog does not do all of these terrible things like biting visitors, destroying your home or killing livestock. Please don't give yourself all the credit for this, because I find that much of a dog's personality comes from random genetic and formative early experiences over which owners had little or no control. Most clients coming to me with a problem pet have previously owned well-behaved dogs that did not need my help. It is all so much the luck of the draw when we take a dog into our lives.

But there is help available out there, and in the UK I can recommend members of the Canine and Feline Behaviour Association (CFBA) for a professional and pragmatic approach to dealing with dogs. By pragmatic, I mean an informed, balanced approach to finding the payoffs and penalties that will change your dog's behaviour for the better.

Bounce with a pupil puppy: adult dogs can be a model for good behaviour and also for unwanted responses such as jumping in the pool. There is no one way to treat or resolve all the behavioural problems in dogs.

7 The Truth about Food

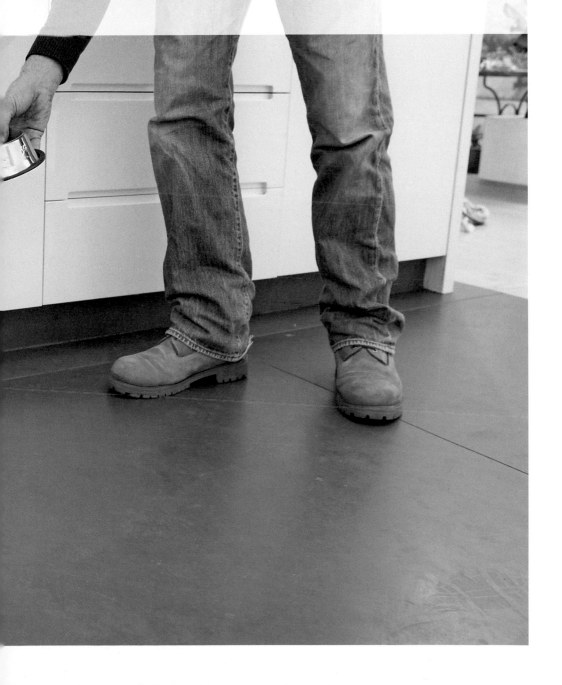

Feeding behaviour, theory and practice

The Truth about Food

The facts about modern pet food and why it isn't doing your dog any good. Healthy alternatives: 'Bones and Raw Food' or doing it yourself. What to do about a problem eater. Obesity in dogs. What to have on your shopping list. Some do's and don'ts to keep your dog healthy.

Canine nutrition is not nearly as complicated as some pet-food manufacturers would have you believe. It is not rocket science, yet just as many people have lost the skills and knowledge required to prepare their own food, so have many dog owners given up on preparing food at home for their pets. This chapter will show that this trend away from home preparation has been bad for dogs and probably bad for our wallets too.

Modern Pet Food

The last 50 years have seen a dramatic shift in the way dogs are fed in Europe, the US, Asia and indeed everywhere. The manufacture of dog food is now a vast business that operates on a global scale. Four multi-national corporations dominate the production and marketing of pet food worldwide; they have virtually hijacked the role that used to be occupied by caring pet owners. Long gone are the days when food for the dog was blended with as much skill as any meal intended for the human family. Now, we have been persuaded to pour sticky stews from a can or unappetizing pellets from a sack into our dogs' bowls. It is a trend that I and many others want to see reversed, for the sake of dogs.

'The manufacture of dog food is now a vast business that operates on a global scale'

Dinner time is an important time to reinforce the hierarchy of the family unit. If one dog finishes their food before another, they should be taught to wait in a 'sit' until the other pets have finished theirs.

Perhaps even more importantly, by delegating responsibility for feeding our pets to major corporations, we have lost something very special in our man-dog relationships. The preparing and giving of food should be an act of nurturing, giving us pride that we're doing the best for our friend, who in return shows his appreciation through anticipation and then enjoyment of food.

Inside the Industry

I spent nine years working for a large pet-food corporation and saw at first hand how the industry works. Historically, tinned food offerings from the major companies have been made to look and smell like home-made stews and have a similar texture. This offers a creative challenge for food technologists: to turn cheap and unappetizing ingredients such as soya (textured vegetable protein), blood and udders into something that looks remarkably like real diced meat. Colorants are added to darken the artificial chunks if it is a 'beef' recipe, or to lighten them if it is a 'chicken' variety. The way it looks and smells to us has become a more important facet of dog food than satisfaction of our animals' nutritional needs.

Artificial flavours are essential if a dog is to gulp down his food at a speed that will impress his naive but doting owners. This is where the clever 'food and flavour' chemists have cracked the code of naturally attractive aromas that come from, say, roast beef or lamb. These are often based on technological fixes such as the complex chemistry of so-called maillard reactions between sugars and sulphur – containing amino

Myth-Busting: Reading the Label Doesn't Necessarily Help

One of the major problems with modern dog food is that we don't know what we are buying. The ingredients are usually cleverly disguised behind such mysterious terms as 'meat and animal derivatives' (what can that mean?!) or 'derivatives of vegetable origin' (which could cover just about anything). Have a look at the label on the can or packet you have recently purchased. Are the species of meat and the organs used mentioned? Probably not. Within the EC there is no legal requirement for it. Nor do manufacturers have to specify which cereals they use – yet, as we shall see later in the chapter – 'derivatives of vegetable origin' can exert a wide range of nutritional and ultimately behavioural effects on dogs.

Pet-food labelling in the United States is more heavily regulated and honest than in Europe; American manufacturers work to a protocol known as AFCO when making claims such as 'complete nutrition' or 'suitable for pregnant bitches and growing puppies'. But within the EC the pet-food industry has done a great job of hoodwinking the consumer regulators, while governments have been persuaded to let the industry regulate itself. Big mistake!

Feel free to give your dog treats, but vary them so that he has a range of textures, smells and palatibility.

Myth-Busting: What Goes Into Those 'Meaty Chunks'

The cheapest ingredient of all is water. Some brands of canned food are more than 80 per cent water, but they are made to look like solid nutrition: the water has been bound up by mostly indigestible gel systems extracted from such foods as seaweed, fruits and tropical beans. These bind water into a stiff jelly which, to all appearances, is a nutritious gravy wrapped around chunks of meat. In reality, they are a device to turn water into… money for the manufacturers! They give no benefit to pets or their people.

acids, which smell nice to a carnivore but do nothing for his nutrition. The flavours are a hoax that fool dogs into eating ingredients that they would not normally eat, such as soya beans.

Cat food is even more profitable to manufacture than tinned dog food and the unhealthy state of cats' teeth and gums can be directly attributed to unsuitable commercial offerings. Mummified Egyptian cat skeletons in the British Museum show that the pharaohs' cats had healthier mouths than their modern counterparts! Gingivitis, stomatitis, rampant calculus, bad breath and chronically infected gums are the price that contemporary dogs and cats pay for our giving them unnatural food. I am very glad to no longer be a part of that industry.

The Truth about Dry Dog Food

Dry dog food is manufactured in a high-pressure, high-temperature extrusion 'gun', in which a slurry of cereals and animal parts are forced down a giant barrel, then pop out from a tiny aperture to become a pellet of dog food. The pellet is not a solid lump; rather it expands by being puffed up with air to more than double the volume of its solid ingredients. Just as tinned dog foods are 'thinned' with water, so are extruded dry foods given the misleading volume: value treatment with cheap air.

One of the many problems besetting both canned and dry dog foods is that the ingredients are all too often dried in factories that could be half a world away from where the food is manufactured. Meats are rendered, bones milled and blood dried so that they can be stored economically and then shipped to distant factories. (High-value meats may be frozen and used to manufacture tinned food, but they are rarely incorporated into dry dog food.) Unsurprisingly, the over-processing of key ingredients in dry foods creates massive losses to their nutritional quality, so that by the time the pellet finally ends its journey down the extruder, it has been stripped of important heat-sensitive enzymes, vitamins and essential oils. The industry gets round this by adding back vitamin supplements, essential oils such as Omega 3 and Omega 6, and antioxidants.

Carnivores have to have certain essential oils in their diet because they cannot manufacture their own. But imagine the damage to these complex and unstable fats if they have been subjected to drying and storage, then dramatic if brief cooking in a dry dog-food plant. Much the same damage is inflicted during the canning process, when these crucial ingredients are supercooked in retorts (giant pressure cookers) at 120°C (250°F) for about an hour.

Worst of all is that the mixing then extrusion of multiple ingredients disguises what these ingredients are. I mentioned earlier that you cannot rely on what you read on the label. Dogs are carnivores, with the teeth and short

'The over-processing of key ingredients in dry foods creates massive losses to their nutritional quality'

alimentary canal that goes with their predatory, meat-eating past. In the wild they do not graze on wheat, maize or soya beans. Dingoes and wolves eat the whole carcass of their prey, preferring some parts to others. Their giant canine teeth are designed to rip through skin and muscle, shredding it so that it can be swallowed without chewing. The sharp cusps of their premolars provide a cutting and crushing platform for dealing with bones. Take away the need for a dog to use his teeth by feeding him mushy wet or powdery dry food and he might

Wild canids usually eat every scrap of their prey. Their teeth are designed to tear flesh and crunch bones, not gulp down a shapeless mush.

Giving your dog raw bones, and other chewy items is an excellent way to keep his teeth and gums healthy.

as well be toothless. Perhaps that is the way for dogs in the future, or perhaps we can stop the downward spiral and return to feeding our domestic predators on natural diets closer to those of their wild ancestors.

There Is Another Way

As a dog owner, you have to take responsibility for what your dog is fed. The purchasing and blending of key ingredients has never been easier than it is today, and there are now many specialist pet stores that provide all you need to create a healthier natural diet. In Canada, for instance, many pet stores offer a fantastic variety of frozen meats and bones, from fish to bison,

A Return to Raw Food

How best to feed dogs has become a controversial area, and much of the credit for stirring things up must go to two Australian veterinarians, Drs Ian Billinghurst and Tom Lonsdale. Billinghurst has popularized the feeding of bones and raw food ('BARF') to dogs because, he argues, it is a return to the natural way to which the wild ancestors of dogs adapted their digestive physiology and their behaviour. The fact that our dogs survive on the artificial diets of industrially packaged or canned pet foods does not mean that they provide optimum nutrition. Rather, they are a compromise built on the pursuit of profit for the manufacturer and the lazy love affair of owners with convenience.

Lonsdale, in his excellent book *Raw Meaty Bones*, takes a determined and well-informed swipe at the pet-food industry, noting

that it has created a virtual epidemic of periodontal disease (inflammation of the gums and other structures supporting the teeth) among cats and dogs. The industry has rather cleverly brought the veterinary profession 'on side', to the extent that vets in practice now positively promote the very foods that create the dental disease they are paid to treat, but too often not to prevent. It is a mutually profitable alliance that Lonsdale has bravely sought to expose and to correct. As a result, he has been denigrated by his professional colleagues who (rightly) regard him as a dangerous prophet of nutritional common sense and object to his rocking the boat of veterinary orthodoxy.

The digestive systems of dogs are designed for meat, not for carb-rich industrial pet foods.

Obesity in Dogs

Today's epidemic of obesity among dogs is a problem of our own making. The high-fat and high-carbohydrate diets too many of us feed our dogs induce (surprise, surprise) obesity! And in addition to causing the periodontal disease mentioned above, those carbohydrates ferment in the stomach and large bowel to induce bloat (a painful and potentially fatal gaseous distension of the stomach) and trigger diabetes, just as a sugary, high-carb diet causes harm to people. This is a complicated catalogue of disasters for the modern dog. Surely the results of bad (human) nutrition that we see all around us should act as a warning that we must do better for dogs and cats than we have for ourselves?

---

ostrich and deer. All are neatly packaged, along with fresh veggies such as spinach. The same trend is underway in the UK and US, though there are fewer converts to BARF here than in Canada or Australia, where it all started (see page 136).

I have so often seen the benefits to dogs that have been switched to a natural diet. They are brighter, their mouths are healthier and tartar-free, faeces are smaller, firmer and less smelly. Owners often report that the unpleasant 'doggy' smell of pets maintained on high-carbohydrate diets quickly disappears, which reflects a changed bacterial population in their sebaceous glands and overall improved dermatological health.

Many of the ingredients that you would happily eat can also go into your dog's dinner bowl.

Dog Dinner Recipes

Dogs like variety, which is a good reason for you to be inventive and to vary the types of animal proteins you feed them if, like me, you have decided to go the natural route. Your local pet store should be your first port of call to find the raw meats that I am suggesting, and then there is your butcher, fishmonger or supermarket. At weekends or in the evenings, supermarkets often have reduced-price offers of nearly date-expired meats. The disadvantage of supermarkets is that they tend not to sell bones, whereas butchers and pet stores do.

And then there is the veg. I am a keen 'grow-my-own', self-sufficiency person, and surplus veg are great for dogs. Greens such as cabbage and spinach can be lightly steamed before being mixed in (you might usefully invest in a blender). Carrots are great raw, possibly grated, but potatoes must be cooked. Go easy on potatoes, though, as with any form of carbohydrate.

Table scraps can form a tasty part of a planned, natural diet: discarding them is such a waste of food and will deny your best friend the pleasure of having a little of what takes his master's fancy. The one item that all pundits agree must be excluded from a dog's diet is cooked bones. They become brittle with sharp edges that can obstruct or even penetrate the gut lining. Raw bones are safe, but if you have a gulping dog who turns every meal into a race against the clock, then supervise him carefully when he is eating bones and give him larger rather than smaller pieces to work on.

Reports from veterinarians caring for BARF-fed dogs suggest that the incidence of gastro-intestinal obstructions caused by bones is no different from that in dogs fed industrial diets.

Some Dos and Don'ts

Returning your dog to a natural way of feeding is almost certain to be beneficial, but there are still some important things to bear in mind. These are some of the questions I am most often asked with reference to a dog's diet.

Isn't there a Risk of Infection with Raw Meat?

It is a near certainty that intensively reared broiler chickens will carry salmonella and/or campylobacter infections. These do not present a hazard to dogs, which are remarkably resistant to a wide range of food-spoiling bacteria: having evolved as predators and carrion-eaters, they are blessed with a robust digestive system. It is nigh impossible to harm a dog with 'off' meat.

However, humans are much more susceptible in this respect, so be careful to segregate the dog's meat from food intended for your own consumption and wash your hands after handling it. If space and budget allow, reduce the risk of cross-contamination by using a separate freezer for dog food and feed him outdoors.

Why Won't All Meat Do?

An all-meat diet is deficient in a range of critical minerals, especially calcium, hence the importance of balancing the proportions of meat and bone to about 2:1 by weight.

Things to Buy

Wherever possible, buy whole carcasses or meat that is on the bone. An all-meat diet will be deficient in calcium and other essential minerals that bones provide. So your shopping list should include:

- Whole carcasses of chicken, turkey and rabbit, and whole fish.
- Poultry by-products such as wings, necks, even feet, heads and skeleton after the main cuts of meat have been removed for human consumption.
- Bones! Any bones from lamb, beef, pork or deer. The large long bones can be a challenge to a little dog, so saw big bones into small pieces. Oxtail is excellent for dogs to chew on, having lots of connective tissue and sinew intertwined with muscle blocks.
- Offal such as a lung, trachea, heart or tripe is fine as long as it does not make up more than a third of the overall diet. Liver is an excellent source of vitamins A and D, but should not form more than 10 per cent of the total diet: in the long term too much of these vitamins (hypervitaminosis) may produce a number of unpleasant symptoms such as weight loss or pain in the joints; and in the short term, liver is likely to cause diarrhoea.

What about Supplements?

If you are feeding a raw and meaty bone diet according to my specifications, there should be no need to supplement it with vitamins and minerals: raw food which has not been heat-processed provides all the nutrients a dog requires. However, live probiotics (benign bacteria that populate a dog's mouth and gut) are beneficial to both natural and industrial diets. Specific medical conditions such as arthritis may respond to the same glucosamine and chondroitin supplements that generally help dogs on industrial diets. By and large, there are greater dangers from over-supplementation if you feed your dog the natural way; 'complete' industrial dog foods are only stuffed with supplements because they are based on bizarre ingredients and processed to the point of near destruction.

combined vitamin and mineral supplements can be obtained from pet stores and there are many good natural sources of essential fatty acids (see What About Fats?, opposite).

How Often Should I Feed My Dog?

This is very much a matter of personal preference: dogs will adapt to a wide range of feeding regimes, from frequent small snacks to a once-per-day gorged meal. It is for you to judge what suits him best. In nature, predators do not have a steady and predictable supply of food: rather there will be dramatic swings

'Dogs will adapt to a wide range of feeding regimes, from frequent small snacks to a once-per-day gorged meal'

If you are worried about sourcing micro-ingredients such as vitamins, zinc or getting the critical calcium:phosphorus ratio just right, don't be! Feeding a variety of meats, bone and vegetables will minimize the risks of your pet running into any long-term nutritional deficiency, and in the short term he is well-buffered to cope with day-to-day variations in intake. Weeks or more are needed to provoke significant nutritional deficiencies in dogs, as also in people. If necessary, inexpensive

between feast and famine. Your dog is capable of making the same physiological and behavioural adaptations to missing one or even several meals, if he has to.

Do Dogs Need a Constant Diet, and Does a Sudden Change Upset Them?

Dogs in the wild are faced with frequent changes because of changing availability of prey species and the different body parts that they eat. Most domestic dogs cope very well with day-to-day

---

Case Study: **The Royal Corgis**

In 1985 I was consulted by the Queen at Windsor Castle about the behaviour of her corgis. She fed her 11 dogs for me to observe in her private apartment. A member of staff wheeled in an enormous tray with 11 rather tasteful bowls, some in silver and others battered by long use, with food freshly prepared in the royal kitchens. No dog was fed the same as

another, and most had 'special' additions such as seaweed, vegetables, oils or homeopathic remedies according to the dog's age or condition. Her Majesty's overriding concern was that each dog should be fed in a way that met its individual needs. And I figure that if home cooking is good enough for the Queen's dogs, it is good enough for yours and mine!

Home-cooked dog food, such as rice and cheap cuts of meat, is satisfying for you to prepare and good for your dog.

changes in diet because their evolutionary past equipped them for life as hunters and scavengers, but they do have to be conditioned to raw foods if they have been used to eating industrial food. In particular, individual brands of extruded dry foods tend to foster a particular gut microbiology, perhaps because they are high in fermentable carbohydrates, which are not present in a natural diet. Supplementary probiotics make adaptation to these variations in commercial diets easier, and also help when switching to a more natural, home-prepared diet.

What About Fats?

In moderation, dogs need fat, just as humans do. However, 'moderation' is the key word here: trim and discard any excess. At the other end of the scale, lean rabbit meat does not provide sufficient fat, so needs to be supplemented. Good sources of essential fatty acids are fish oils (such as salmon oil), evening primrose oil, olive oil and others that are sold for human consumption. The nutritional requirements of our two species are remarkably similar, so if it is good enough for you, it should be good enough for him. The exception is chocolate, which is poisonous to

dogs because of its theobromine content, and for different reasons grapes and raisins must be strictly reserved for human consumption.

Is a Raw Meaty Diet Suitable for Growing Puppies and Breeding Bitches?

Pregnancy and lactation impose specific and demanding nutritional requirements. In principle, a BARF diet can sustain breeding bitches and growing puppies, but it must be carefully planned. Consult your vet for specific advice about your dog's nutritional needs.

The Home-Cooked Alternative

Dogs throughout the ages have thrived on the scraps and kitchen creations of their people. British and American dog owners were the first to be hooked by the seductive messages of the pet-food marketeers, whereas French, Italian and Asian consumers are late converts, perhaps because their food cultures were stronger than in English-speaking countries. When I interviewed French pet owners in the 1970s, I found that most of them had a healthy scepticism about industrial dog foods, preferring to concoct recipes at home from the same ingredients they used to feed the family. Rice was the carb of choice, meat was selected on a daily basis from what was cheap at the butcher or fish merchant, and herbs or natural flavourings were chosen to suit the cook's palate and to indulge what experience had shown Fifi enjoyed. Those French dogs looked just fine on their culinary creations, and so do most dogs fed on sensibly balanced, mixed ingredients that have been creatively cooked at home.

'The important point to make is that there is no one right way to feed dogs: there are many'

How different it is in France today, where they are as likely to purchase *les boites* or *croquettes* (tinned and dry food) as the rest of the world, and it is the same story of capitulation to the multi-national dog-food companies in food-conscious Italy and Asia. More is the pity!

The important point to make is that there is no one right way to feed dogs: there are many, because they are very adaptable creatures who have succeeded alongside humans because of that flexibility. Their digestive system is well suited to being totally carnivorous but it can, if needs be, even adapt to a carefully blended vegetarian diet. The 'in between' state of a home-prepared, mixed meat and veg omnivorous diet may be the practical and economical alternative to BARF, and will in all likelihood be better for both of you than the industrial alternative. So there is no need to feel guilty if 100 per cent BARF does not suit your lifestyle, your pocket or even your dog. Some dogs really seem to prefer the taste and smell of cooked meat, but you should know that a natural raw diet is, overall, the healthier alternative for your pet.

Industrial Alternatives to BARF

Aside from the big four multi-national companies mentioned at the beginning of the chapter, there are literally hundreds of small, independent manufacturers of dog food. How can you be sure that one diet is better than another? The marketeers of dry foods claim that theirs is more 'premium' than another and try to catch your eye and your wallet with claims that they contain special ingredient X, Y or Z – perhaps New Zealand green-lipped mussels, exotic seaweeds or organically produced meats from humanely raised animals.

The biggest problem with all dried extruded diets is that they have to contain high levels of cereal for the physical process to work: superheated carbs are needed to chemically bond with the proteins. But as I said earlier, cereals are not found in the diet of wild dogs, and wheat in particular is high in gluten, to which many dogs are intolerant or even allergic. Rice and especially white (milled) rice is low in gluten and is more suitable for feeding to dogs. Oats are also an excellent alternative to wheat and provide a source of soluble fibre (good for their digestive system), together with other health benefits well known to Scottish readers. A good ingredient for industrial dog foods, cooked rice or rolled oats can also be incorporated into home recipes by owners not choosing the total BARF route.

The Importance of Tryptophan

Another cereal to avoid is corn (maize), which provides notably low levels of tryptophan. Tryptophan is used in the body to manufacture brain serotonin, a chemical that is known to promote calmness. It has been claimed (but not definitely substantiated) that diets which are low in tryptophan adversely affect moods in dogs, as they have been experimentally shown to increase fear and other emotional responses in rodents. One of the several paradoxes of the veterinary connection to industrial dog foods is that one high-profile, multi-national manufacturer of 'clinical' diets, which are sold almost exclusively through veterinarians, uses recipes whose sole carbohydrate source is corn. The same manufacturer has pared down the protein levels to the experimentally-determined bare minimum for canine survival, but of course maize is so much cheaper than meat!

You will soon find whether or not a particular commercial diet suits your dog: just monitor his stools, coat, mouth, body odour, activity levels and overall contentedness. Most dogs seem to get by in the short term on the industrial foods I have been so critical of. However, a minority undergo dramatic behavioural changes when they are fed the 'wrong' diet (see box below). Just as some children and adults are sensitive to, say, shellfish or nuts, so are some dogs allergic to ingredients that the majority tolerate. The lesson here is, 'Feed your dog as an individual, not as an 'average' animal.'

Allergies and Hypersensitivities

Individual dogs, like people, can have dramatic adverse reactions to certain foods or ingredients. I regularly explore these possibilities with dogs whose temperament varies from day to day, sometimes mellow and even lethargic, the next moment threatening and hyperactive.

The basis of these hypersensitivities is poorly understood but we can often correlate behavioural reactions to particular diets with responses of the immune system. It may be that an affected dog cannot tolerate a particular protein source, a carbohydrate, a colorant or even, in one case, the protective lacquer that is painted on the inside of dog cans.

We explore these dietary sensitivities by providing a 'clean' exclusion diet made up of:

- one part boiled white meat such as chicken, white fish or rabbit
- one part boiled white rice, oats or mashed potato
- one tablespoon olive oil per 10 kg (22 lb) body weight.

I recommend feeding each meat/carbohydrate combination for a one-week period while monitoring changes to the dog's skin, coat condition or faeces – and hopefully finding improvements in behaviour. If there is no change, we might vary the source of carbs or protein and test for another week.

When we find an exclusion diet that gives positive results, we can design a long-term maintenance regime. In my practice, it will usually be to switch the dog to BARF, adding bonemeal, other minerals and oils as required. My experience is that dogs 'allergic' to foods are usually reacting to specific but unknown ingredients in commercial dog foods, best avoided by preparing their meals at home, just as a good parent has to get involved in what his or her children eat.

Preparing your dog's food at home yourself gives you control over the choice of ingredients.

Adding water to dried food reliably makes it more palatable.

The Convenience Factor

Industrial dried dog food does offer advantages to owners, if not to their dogs. It is convenient, clean and can be stored for long periods without the expense of having a freezer. It is also easy to calculate how much to feed your dog to keep him at his ideal weight. On average, a dried dog food provides 300 calories per 100 g (85 calories per ounce). A medium-sized dog of average activity requires about 60 calories of energy per kilo of body weight (27 calories per pound). By this formula, a 20kg (44lb) dog will expend approximately 1,200 calories, requiring an intake of 400g (14oz) of dried food a day. However, there are vast individual differences that affect this calculation, such as sex, activity levels, age and other variations in metabolic rate.

Some of the problems inherent in dry dog food can be lessened. Certain manufacturers have begun to substitute potato for cereals in extruded diets, which is not so liable to produce the fermentable sugars that can cause dental and gastrointestinal problems. Another technological fix is that instead of being extruded at high temperatures and pressures, the food can be gently pasteurized and cold-pressed. The result can be a somewhat unsightly hard cube that looks rather like the commercial diets used to feed farm animals, but at least its production has caused less damage to the delicate enzymes and other heat-sensitive proteins, fats and vitamins.

A German company, Markus Muhle, has perfected the art of extruding dog diets at a temperature of only 30–34°C (86–93°F), which produces tangible nutritional benefits. Their approach does not puff up the food with air – rather it creates a solid chunk that rapidly breaks down in the dog's stomach. I became convinced of the benefits of the cold-extrusion system by the simple test of placing a few pellets of extruded dry food into a glass of water, where it swelled into near-permanent and semi-solid gelatinous lumps. Try the experiment yourself and imagine that in your dog's stomach! The cold-pressed alternative reacts to soaking in water very differently, breaking down within a short time into fine particles and offering a large surface area on which gut enzymes can work.

Despite such small advances in the technology of producing industrial dry dog foods, I still recommend that you consider the first principles of canine nutrition and acknowledge that your dog evolved from a wild predator who had to use his intelligence, speed and skill to catch prey. Feeding your dog should be much more interesting than just depositing a homogenous mash onto a plate; rather food should be something that is healthy or at least does not provoke disease, can be enjoyed slowly and enhances the bond between you.

Feeding Problems

Food and feeding practices are the key building blocks for optimum behavioural husbandry and health in dogs, just as they are for people. But even with best practice, problems can still arise. The three commonest feeding problems about which I am consulted are the greedy feeder, the fussy feeder and the speedy feeder.

The Greedy Feeder

You never see a fat wolf, coyote or dingo in the wild, even when prey is plentiful during the Arctic summer or in Australia after an explosion in rabbit numbers. Wild dogs seem to do better at regulating their waistlines than their domestic counterparts. We have to take responsibility for managing our dogs' diets so they do not become fat, which for a Labrador owner, for example, can be quite a challenge! Here are the key features of a good weight-control programme:

eased off his sofa and into a more frequent and physically demanding exercise regime. If his joints are rickety, be gentle about getting him back into shape with exercise. Consider joining a canine hydrotherapy club or use one of the several excellent designs of canine treadmills on which steady aerobic exercise can be maintained without placing damaging strain on joints and muscles.

- Foster the work ethic: nothing in life should come free! Wild predators have to work to

'Food should be something that can be enjoyed slowly and enhances the bond between you'

- Little and often: multiple meals are better than a large meal once a day.
- Dilute the calories, adding fibre to the dog's diet by introducing vegetables. Try boiled or raw carrot, greens and even young grasses or herbs.
- Cut out the carbs. Carbohydrates alone are a reason to stop feeding industrial food and switch to a BARF diet.
- Expend more calories: exercise! The proverbial canine couch potato must be

hunt and kill prey, and you should try to devise a little of the same for your domestic predator. People who work in zoos and labs refer to this as environmental enrichment: food is hidden, buried or placed in specially designed receptacles that the animal must roll, squeeze or drop to dislodge food. Pet stores sell many such gadgets, which provide

A Kong toy or similar food-dispensing device will encourage your dog to work for his calories!

slow delivery of dry dog food. You can achieve the same effects by scattering dry food over the lawn so your dog has to hunt for it; what he misses can be taken by the birds. Bury bones in woodchip or under leaves in the garden, or position small bowls of wet food strategically around the garden, covering them with old

The Fussy Feeder

About 10 per cent of domestic dogs can fairly be described as difficult feeders, meaning that they reject much of what is put before them or that they eat very slowly. These so-called inappetent dogs may be thin, but a surprising number of fussy feeders have a normal body weight or

'Dogs that gulp down their food cannot possibly savour the subtle features of flavour or texture'

towels and sheets that the dog has to pull off before he gains access to the food. Use your imagination to create challenging situations that your dog solves by his efforts and applied intelligence.

Cleverly designed feeders such as this one slow down feeding and reduce the risk of gastric torsion in vulnerable breeds.

are even fat. Such dogs have found a way of ransoming their owners to please and appease their drive for ever more palatable and indulgent recipes. Some breeds are more likely to present these challenges than others: fussiness tends to affect skinny breeds such as whippets and also some toy breeds such as poodles, but rarely Labradors!

If you own a fussy feeder, your first step should be to discuss the situation with your veterinarian: it may be that your idea of the dog's ideal body weight is unrealistic and that a slim dog carrying no excess fat is actually in good shape. I and most canine professionals would rather that dogs be slim than fat. If you are right to be worried, here are some tricks of my behavioural trade.

- Social facilitation: feed him alongside another dog. There is nothing quite like competition to stimulate interest in food.
- Make the food more palatable. Industrial dry dog food can be boring, but the mere addition of water greatly improves its palatability. Warm it or add grated cheese, strips of biltong

or other natural flavour enhancers. Cooking makes meat more palatable for dogs just as it does for people, so you may have to give up on the raw aspect of the BARF approach.

- Gorge feed. This is the opposite strategy to my recommendation for the greedy feeder. Give your picky eater one or at most two meals per day, then remove uneaten food rather than leaving it for 'grazing' through the day.
- High-energy food is good. Add fats of animal or vegetable origin and reduce non-nutritive fibre such as are in green veg. (He can do without it in the short term.)
- Eat together: change your dog's feeding time to your main meal time, so that he benefits from the aroma and social goings-on of a family dinner. In the wild, packs of dogs all feed together, because their hunting success is a group achievement rather than the result of an individual enterprise.

The Speedy Feeder: Eat Slowly!

Dogs that gulp their food down cannot possibly savour the subtle features of flavour or texture that we would like to see enjoyed by our gourmandizing canine companion. Just as the healthy and fashionable way for us to eat is slowly, so it should be for our dogs. Here is a way to slow down eating and hopefully to teach him to enjoy his food more, with less risk of regurgitating or even experiencing life-threatening bloat.

- Slow is good. If you are feeding a raw, natural diet, give him larger chunks and not finely chopped bits separate from the bone. Avoid sloppy and easily eaten wet foods.
- Freeze! Freezing food is an excellent way to make a dog develop inventive eating strategies. He may lick it, or perhaps chew frozen wet foods. Dry foods can be moistened and then frozen.

A monthly weight check is good practice. Obesity is the modern killer disease of dogs.

- Make it difficult for him to eat quickly. There are many designs of bowl which force dogs to eat more slowly. A very effective DIY remedy is to place two or more pebbles in your dog's bowl so that he has to push them aside to get at the food. The Danish inventor Ni Liu has taken this concept to another level with her 'green' feeding bowl concept (See left).

In Summary

In summary, dogs are easy, adaptable animals to feed and there are many ways in which only fair nutritional standards can be met. But in my opinion dogs survive on most industrial diets; if they are to thrive and live a better, more contented life, they need something more interesting than bland offerings in a sack. Engaging in good feeding practices is probably the single most significant contribution you can make to enhancing the welfare of your dog.

8 Lifestyle & Needs

Accommodating behaviour

Lifestyle & Needs

Dogs need routine, but they also need to fit in with changes in your life. What to do with them when you are out at work or on holiday. Ensuring their safety when you move house. Introducing your dog to a new baby. And finally, inevitably, helping him deal with going to the vet's.

Textbooks about farm animals have whole sections devoted to the content and timing of feed, the floor surfaces on which they walk, when they are mated, stocking density and so on. Get it wrong and you can expect cows to produce less milk, chickens to die or horses to go lame. The pet dog is an extraordinary exception because there is no one agreed system to satisfy his physical and psychological needs or to ensure that he is happy and healthy. Nor should there be any such set of rules because, as we know, dogs are amazingly adaptable creatures, living in terrains from Arctic cold to desert heat and

throughout history coping with massive changes in human lifestyles and our diverse cultures.

This adaptability should make you suspicious of any author or 'expert' who proposes hard and fast rules on how you should care for your dog. The mere preference of a dog for, say, warmth in winter or cool in summer does not mean that you have to invest in a near-tropical central-heating system or in air-conditioning. Dogs are quite capable of so-called behavioural thermo-regulation, seeking out shade and damp when it is hot or, in the winter, huddling together, fluffing coats for insulation and avoiding draughts. More

'Dogs are capable of seeking out shade when it is hot or, in the winter, huddling together and avoiding draughts'

Despite what is often said about the natural animosity between cats and dogs, they can be good companions for each other and resolve the loneliness problem that sometimes arises when you have to leave them alone.

important than these physical wants is a dog's need for a stable and loving relationship with people, with other dogs and, in our pet-loving culture, with other species as well.

In this chapter, I will be introducing the concept of behavioural husbandry, meaning the resources and routines that dogs require in order to cope with modern life. How can you make your dog's time alone in the house more tolerable when you are at work? If you move from country to town, how will the country dog cope with city noises, smells and polluted busy parks? Maybe you are expecting a baby and need to ensure that the relationship between your dog and your child is happy and risk-free. Then, finally, there is the important issue of veterinary care, and how you can apply good principles of behavioural husbandry to help your dog cope with those unavoidable visits to the vet's.

The Working Pet Parent and Home-Alone Dog

If you find that your dog is distressed when you are out of the house, there are several options available. First, consider having a second dog – or perhaps a cat; many a cat-dog partnership is as fulfilling as a two-dog pairing. Acquiring a second or third pet is not something to be undertaken lightly, so you might sensibly 'borrow' a dog that you know to be friendly with yours and see how it works out. Only if you are sure that the companionship of another animal will please your dog should you set out to find a new puppy or adopt a rescue dog.

Alternatively, assuming that it isn't possible for you to work from home, you might negotiate with your employer about taking your dog to work. Many work environments are pet-friendly, allowing dogs to lie quietly under their owner's

Myth-Busting: Your Dog Doesn't Just Sleep While You're Out

Does he drift into contented sleep or have a miserable time waiting for your return? You can answer this question by setting up a camcorder or a webcam to see what your dog does in your absence. I have viewed many such film records and know that most dogs do not enjoy the contented sleep you would like to imagine. Rather, they pace and whine and don't play with the toys you have so thoughtfully left for them. Heart rate and blood pressure usually rise dramatically when the owner leaves, then after 15–30 minutes they drop to near or below normal levels. Typically, a home-alone dog lies still for five or ten minutes and may then have occasional panic attacks, pacing and perhaps entering a bedroom to sniff his owner's clothes. During these brief periods of activity, heart rate and blood pressure surge, before returning to

normal or depressed levels as he lies down in what may look to you like a sad, grieving state.

Methods to alleviate loneliness are described in Chapter 6, where I emphasize the importance of preliminary exercise, food-dispensing activity toys and access to favourite areas of the house. And of course there are happy exceptions – dogs that are less dependent on human company relax and may even enjoy the opportunity to catch up on their sleep. But such dogs have probably been 'trained' to separation by being raised in kennels by their breeder or in a rescue centre. Is it better to have a dog that loves you but suffers for his love, or one that is independent? Of course, the ideal is to find a compromise that optimizes the dog's welfare when he is alone yet still means he needs and enjoys your company when you are home.

How Long Can a Dog be Left Alone?

Many re-homing organizations will not allow anyone to adopt a dog if they are out of the house for more than half a day. The rationale is that dogs are social creatures and should not be left alone for long periods. I sympathize with that view and, of course, puppies should not be left alone for long during their critical stages of early development. But it should not be imposed as a hard and fast rule where adult dogs are concerned. We have all, from time to time, been obliged to leave our dog for longer than four or five hours and have returned to find that he is seemingly fine, especially if he has canine company and a friend or neighbour has dropped by. After all, many rescue dogs are cooped up for long periods, having a poorer quality of life than they will experience in an 'at home' situation. Many of my clients would have liked to adopt a rescue dog but have been turned down on the grounds of having an unsuitable lifestyle. They then go on to buy a puppy, with the unintended consequence that fewer adult dogs get to be re-homed and more puppies are brought to market to fulfil people's passion for the company of animals.

desk or work bench. My experience is that a well-managed dog in the workplace improves team morale in multiple subtle ways. For instance, visitors often begin their conversation by enquiring about the dog rather than the boss. Or when things are tough, a dog can act as a social mediator, a confidant and an uncritical friend in a way that the professional from HR cannot.

Dog Day-Care

If you do have to be out all day, day-care is a great option, popular in North America and catching on in the UK and elsewhere. The dog is dropped off just like a child attending kindergarten and is then supervised to live and play in small groups with other dogs of compatible size, temperament and activity levels. Most managers of dog day-care facilities insist that their 'guests' are neutered (to reduce fighting) and will turn away aggressive animals. When looking for a suitable day-care centre, check that there are lots of play opportunities, on-leash walks, and sleeping facilities in individual cubicles where your dog can recover.

You may have had a tough day at the office, but he has had a great time at day-care! Of course, day-care can just as easily be provided by a neighbour, relative or friend, who may expect and deserve to be paid for the service.

Employing a Dog Walker

Then there is the up-and-coming profession of dog walking. This is becoming increasingly organized: you will have seen painted vans collecting and delivering dogs across town, taking them to parks and forests for exercise. It sounds great, but there can be drawbacks and dangers. A dog walker must take personal responsibility for the welfare and safe control of the animals left in his or her care. Does he or she have the strength and skills to control one, two, three or more dogs on a walk? Question his credentials, and especially ask other clients how they feel about his care of their pet. Check that he carries full insurance: that is absolutely essential. Finally, ask how many dogs he takes for walks at one time. The maximum should, in my opinion be five, but ideally three or four.

Myth-Busting: Apartment Living Can Be Fine

Practically speaking, the cost of housing dictates where we live and, sadly, the ideal of a fully fenced, 40-hectare (100-acre) horse farm may just not be realizable. The British love their gardens, which are convenient resources for dogs. However, most city dwellers in Japan or Switzerland, not to mention most New Yorkers, Londoners and Parisians, live in apartments with no access to a garden or yard. Can these be suitable places to have a dog?

There is a widespread presumption that living in a flat or apartment is not good for a dog. Dogs need rolling acres and fresh air, don't they? The answer is 'yes', but in most cities there are parks that can provide as good or better exercise opportunities than can be found in suburbia or in the country. No matter what the weather, the dog's toileting needs can be accommodated by supervised trips, armed with poop pick-up bags. Of course coaxing your dog to go out to the garden on a rainy night will always be a more attractive option, but he would probably rather have your company when doing the deed.

Apartment living imposes special hygiene challenges if your dog is elderly and perhaps incontinent. This is where the 'piddle pad' or indoor toilet comes into its own, and there are lots of inventors who have dreamed up flushable indoor dog loos. However, simply laying absorbent materials in a redundant shower tray can be a good way to train a dog to toilet indoors. In Japanese cities, this approach of keeping (usually small) dogs indoors has become the norm, and similar ways of living are developing in other Asian countries such as Korea and China. However, if the dogs were consulted, I expect that they would prefer to have regular walks outdoors, even on city streets.

Many landlords and housing associations place restrictions on the number and type of pets that can be kept, or even forbid the keeping of dogs in apartments. In the United States, these pet bans have been challenged in the federal courts and many cases have been overturned. However, in the less pet-friendly United Kingdom, it is all too common to find that dogs are not allowed in rented housing. You just have to search for somewhere more accommodating or turn on the charm to persuade the landlord that your dog is going to be the perfectly mannered and managed pet.

There is no reason why your dog shouldn't be perfectly happy living in an apartment, as long as you are meticulous about making sure he has enough exercise and frequent 'comfort' outings.

Many public parks limit the number of dogs that may be walked by one person. In my view this is a sensible precaution against human park-users being intimidated by large and unruly packs of dogs.

In London, many of the royal parks limit the number of dogs that may be exercised to three per person, a regulation introduced because visitors were being terrorized by 'packs' of eight or more excited and uncontrolled dogs. Professional dog walkers have to exercise high standards of discipline or your best friend could lose his life.

Moving Home

In the UK, the average time between moves is six years, in the US it is five and getting shorter every year. Packing up and moving is a stressful activity for people, let alone for their pets. Boxes are everywhere, with strangers lifting and moving furniture and changing the layout of the home. This might be a good time to send your dog off to day-care, to a neighbour's or even to boarding kennels. The risk of his being traumatized can be great.

Moving to a new property presents its own challenges, first and foremost being whether or not the garden fences are up to scratch. If they are not, there is a real danger of a dog escaping and getting lost because there are no familiar landmarks to help him find his way home. Think ahead and fix the fences and garden gates before moving in. Fences must be a higher priority than a new kitchen, bathroom or carpets.

Fortunately, most dogs seem to enjoy change and adapting to a new home is probably less challenging than a camping or touring vacation. Hopefully, your new property will give your dog more space, be closer to parks and country walks

Car Travel

Car travel is the most hazardous activity any dog can be exposed to. We all acknowledge the risk to people by investing in passenger-restraint systems and air bags, but what about the dog? A slow collision or even a sudden braking turns him into a missile hurtling forward, potentially injuring both dog and people. In a major collision, doors can burst open and set dogs free on the road. Just as no responsible parent would take a baby in a car without appropriate safety paraphernalia, so it should be with your dog. Road-traffic experts and the police recommend that dogs be either contained within a crash-proof container, securely anchored in the rear of a car, or that they wear a restraint harness.

There are many such harnesses on the market, but don't buy by price alone. The flimsier options are just that and are likely to fail at the critical moment. There are no internationally agreed safety or construction standards for pet-restraint harnesses comparable to car safety belts for people: you have to use your best judgement about the quality of the stitching and strength of attachments to the seat belt or other safe anchorage point in the vehicle.

The 'cool vest' is a sensible investment to for your dog in hot weather, particularly if you are taking him to places where it is difficult to find shade.

and have dog-friendly neighbours! Speaking from considerable experience at resolving local disputes over pets, I cannot overemphasize the importance of researching the prospective folks next door: don't proceed if you might be moving into a dog-hostile neighbourhood. You may love your dog, but you can't expect the rest of the world to share your sentiments.

Vacations

Hotels and vacation homes are increasingly recognizing that we hate to be separated from our pets. Pet-friendly hotels, resorts, campsites and holiday homes can now be located via the Internet. Most impose a modest but justified 'cleaning charge' for pets, and there may be restrictions on where you can and can't take your dog. In Britain and the US, dogs are likely to be banned from hotel restaurants (though they are often welcome at the bar or in an outdoor eating area), because we suffer from the strange delusion that they are insanitary creatures. France and other European destinations are usually more dog-friendly.

Summer vacations by the ocean may sound ideal for a dog, but not if it is hot. You will have seen dogs on shadeless beaches suffering from the heat and desperate for water. The risks of hyperthermia are very real, especially for brachycephalic breeds (those with almost square heads and short muzzles) such as Bulldogs and Boxers. Much better that they be left at home or placed in boarding kennels (see below).

'Hopefully, your new property will give your dog more space and be closer to parks and country walks'

If your dog suffers from the heat – as many do, especially the young, the old and breeds with flat faces – consider buying him a 'cool vest'. This works by being soaked in water, which steadily evaporates keeping the dog cool, while its laminated lining stops him getting wet. In summer, always travel with water containers to keep your dog's vest 'topped up'.

Boarding Kennels

The safe and sensible alternative to taking your dog on holiday is to place him in a boarding kennel where you know he cannot escape. This might be a traumatizing experience for a dog that is used to his home comforts, but should be less so if you introduce him to a kennel when he is a youngster and more adaptable to changes of routine. Boarding kennels in the UK and elsewhere are regulated by local government and inspected to ensure that they achieve minimum standards for space, hygiene, husbandry, staff training and so on. In the UK, you should insist that the kennels show evidence of having received a satisfactory inspection and ideally they should be a member of a professional organization such as the Pet Care Trust Kennel and Cattery Association.

You should meet the individual staff who will be caring for your dog, see his intended kennel and be reassured that he will receive the care that you expect. Ideally, take him for a 24- or 48-hour trial, just to see how he copes before committing to a two-week or longer period of stay. All boarding kennels will insist upon evidence of your dog having up-to-date vaccinations, but policies vary on preventative treatment for kennel cough, which is often imperfect due to the disease having multiple strains. Be sure to leave contact details for you, other family members and, most importantly, his vet.

It is best to take reminders from home such as his bed, bedding and toys and to ensure that he is fed on the same diet he has with you. Hopefully he will not be too stressed by the experience. A well-run kennel need not be a place where dogs engage in desperate barking and other such signs of disturbed, institutional behaviour. Finally, ask if the kennels have a webcam installed so you can see how he is doing while you are away, but be warned, you may be upset by what you see!

Having a Baby

My consultations with pet owners always include psychological exploration of how they see their relationship with their dog or cat. Is it just an animal adjunct to the human family, or is the relationship one of a 'pet parent', where the dog

The Over-Protective Dog

Rather than dogs attacking children of the family, my experience is that many more can be too protective of 'their' child: they will 'see off' people whom they (wrongly) imagine to be a threat. That is a problem to be resolved by, in all likelihood, returning to first principles of canine management and learning (see Chapter 4). Create positive expectations from approaching strangers by using food (the payoff), but with the penalty of reprimand or rejection if the dog threatens the stranger. If in doubt, seek professional advice, and muzzle if there is any risk that the dog might bite.

Better to muzzle your dog than run the risk that he might bite someone in an attempt to protect you.

is treated, talked to and indulged as a child might be? Many of us are in the latter category (I plead guilty!) and it cuts across all age groups: empty nesters are just as likely to treat their pet as a vulnerable infant as younger folks.

However, a 'real' baby coming on the scene means that it is time for a reality check: the clumsy canine will definitely have to improve his manners around a vulnerable infant. Often, parents-to-be harbour anxieties that their dog may 'turn' in a frenzied, jealous attack upon the new arrival, that the cat will smother him in his cot or that the dog will bring disease into the home. Fortunately, in the vast majority of cases, these fears are unfounded, but there are some preliminary behavioural signs to watch out for ahead of baby coming home.

Accustom your dog to young children but always supervise at-risk toddlers.

Is There Likely to Be a Problem?

If any friends or other members of your family already have a baby, take the opportunity to monitor your dog's reactions to it. Does your terrier get wildly excited by the cries of an infant as he does by the squeaks of his favourite toy? Does the dog make threatening stares or worse towards children he encounters in the park or at home? These are pretty obvious warning signals that your ambition for combining pet ownership with parenthood may not, after all, be achievable. However, that is very rarely the outcome for the dog-owning parents who consult me.

What can you do to 'condition' your dog ahead of baby coming home? First and foremost, have a framework of compliance or obedience between you and the dog. Make sure that he sits on command and 'stays' until released. Adapt him to 'stay' in his basket or, if he is crate-trained, to his bed in the crate. Install child gates to separate your dog from places where the baby may be left unattended from time to time. Never allow the dog unsupervised access to a baby, or indeed to any child under the age of, say, ten years.

Take your dog to see friends with young children. Have him sit and seemingly receive

'The clumsy canine will definitely have to improve his manners around a vulnerable infant'

treats and indulgence for being close to them. If they have a baby in a pram or pushchair, accompany them on walks so that, again, his expectation is 'babies bring me good times'!

If, at any stage in these preliminary assessments of your dog, you have doubts, you should of course seek professional advice. Ask your veterinarian to refer you to an experienced trainer or professional behaviourist who has been through the parenting experience themselves and can take a detached, third-party view of your situation.

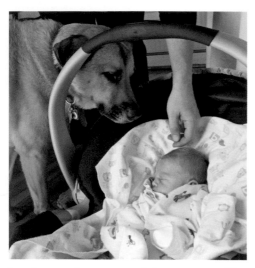

Introduce your dog to your new baby as soon as possible and under careful supervision.

When the Newborn Comes Home

At the moment that you bring home your baby, the dog has to be introduced to his new best friend-to-be. Of course you will be cautious and if there is the hint of a jealous or predatory threat by the dog, now or at any time in the future, you will be even more cautious. The introduction may be a two- or three-person job, with one restraining the dog while the other holds baby within sight but just out of reach. Use that 'sit' response, and from then on try to involve the dog in most of the baby's everyday care routines:

dog accepts his lot as 'canine co-parent'. But both child and dog need constant supervision and even enforced restraint. The big change in the dynamics of the baby-dog relationship comes when baby begins to walk. The moment he rises up onto two feet, he makes a statement that he is not, after all, a weird hairless animal, but rather has attributes remarkably like the rest of humanity. This is the time when the older baby might get him or herself into difficulties, fiddling with the dog's toys or food, or just pulling him about. Many toddlers use their dog as a walking aid and, remarkably, many dogs willingly accept that role. Dogs have strong nurturing instincts that they extend to unrelated puppies in their natural pack situation. It is normal that they should extend the same co-caring instincts to a human baby.

As parents, you have to be vigilant at all times, because at any age things just might go wrong between baby and dog. Stories of a child being mauled by the family pet make media headlines because of their rarity, but they also serve as a salutary warning. If in doubt at any time or in any situation, muzzle the dog when he is around children or, in the worst case scenario, re-home him. That will be a tough decision for any dog lover, but one that a responsible parent must be prepared to take.

'Try to involve the dog in most of the baby's everyday care routines: feeding, washing and play'

feeding, washing and play. Whenever possible take dog and baby on walks together (subject to his not pulling on the lead, see Chapter 4).

Older Babies

Toddlers can do horrible things to dogs but, remarkably, most 'get away with it' because the

On the positive side, the benefit of having a dog with a baby is that pet care exercises the same skills and produces some of the same irritations as parenthood itself; dogs are dirty, require constant attention and thrive when there is a predictable husbandry system. So it is with children! It is when children grow up and make those unaccompanied forays into the woods and parks with their best friend that the child-dog relationship really comes into its own –and indeed comes full circle. From being cared for, the child becomes the carer, exercising benign authority that now protects the dog. Baby grows up and your dog can be a wonderful part of that process.

To the Vet's!

Many dogs hate going to the vet's, just as many of us are anxious at having to go to the dentist. Very early on in a puppy's life the characteristic uniform, the smell of disinfectant, medicines and odours from other stressed dogs form a memory trace that can be difficult to eradicate later. But vets don't deserve all this fear and loathing because, by and large, they are a dog-loving lot! So it is worth investing time and creativity in reducing your dog's unjustified fears. Of course, this has to be done in partnership with your vet and nursing staff. The payoff for the vet will be a more pleasant doctor-patient partnership, less stress and danger from handling a frightened dog. He or she will also obtain a much more realistic insight into the dog's normal behaviour and physical condition if the animal is relaxed. Acute stress markedly affects the clinical indices of underlying disease, such as heart, gut and endocrine function and the results of blood tests.

Your Puppy and the Vet

How can you persuade your dog to enjoy going to the vet's? Of course, the best time to start is when he is a puppy, during that first visit for a health check and shots. It is a consultation that must not be hurried and should include lots of petting, fussing and treating from the vet and nurses. It is really important that the inevitable needle experience is left until the last moment, just as the exit door opens and the puppy is rewarded by the consultation being over. All too often, the consultation is done the other way around, with the nasty bits administered early on and the conversation, fussing and giving of treats coming afterwards. But following an injection, no reward can be as potent as release from pain or escape from the vet's consulting room.

Tellington Touch

Linda Tellington Jones developed the theory and practice for the treatment of a range of disorders in people and in animals. A combination of specific touches, lifts and movement exercises helps release tension, increase body awareness and improve balance. A gentle non-invasive extension of ancient Chinese acupuncture using fingers rather than needles. I have seen some very good outcomes in fearful dogs that lacked the confidence or social skills to deal with other dogs or people. Only consult a TT accredited practitioner, with the correct training.

Solutions for Adult Dogs

Dogs with a long-established fear of going to the vet's will need a planned re-education programme to show that the car park, waiting and examination rooms are not, after all, so threatening. A single painful visit may need dozens of positive experiences to reverse those unpleasant memories. Enlist your vet's help and get permission just to drop in at the surgery when things are quiet and staff have time to offer treats, games and gentle massage, but without formal treatment. Fear of the vet can assume the seriousness of any phobia, and the same principles of phobic desensitization apply: small increments in exposure having consistently rewarding outcomes (see page 108).

The modern concept of pain-free dentistry has revolutionized our attitude to injections and restorative work. The same philosophy is taking hold in the veterinary profession, many of whose members have had training in techniques that put a canine patient at ease in a firm and confident manner, but having respect for the idiosyncratic ways of dogs.

But even with the most pet-friendly vet, there will be some dogs who respond by biting – either the vet or you as you try to restrain him. These dogs need to be pre-trained to accept a muzzle. Do this by introducing one at home, interspersed with all the usual activities that the dog enjoys. Wearing a muzzle must be seen not as something that only happens at the vet's, but rather as a prelude to play before meals and as a price to pay for affection from you. Fortunately, there are now muzzle designs available that allow you to feed your dog a treat while he is wearing one, and these have revolutionized the art and practice of containing dangerous dogs.

The vet may also have to make concessions. Could he wear something other than the clinical uniform that your dog hates? Does the dog have to be lifted on to an examination table – can he not just as well be examined and treated on the floor? Maybe the whole process can be done outside, even in the back of your car. I advise vets to invest time in their patients by taking them for a short walk, throwing a ball, working a squeaky toy and not always acting as a stuffy dog-doctor clinician. These issues are vitally important because there may come a time when a real emergency arises and your dog has to be hospitalized. And as he ages, he will definitely need the skill and friendship of the vet to maintain his quality of life in the final years.

A good vet will invest time in making his patients feel at ease when they come for a medical examination.

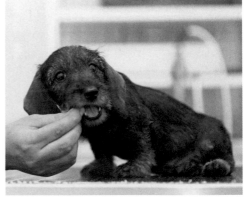

Getting the vet or veterinary nurse to feed your dog treats is another way of helping the consultation go smoothly.

Grooming

Haircare for fluffy or hairy dogs is vital for their health and welfare, but a dog's first visit to a grooming salon could be a scary experience if not handled correctly. The young puppy should be given treats and toys then later introduced to combs, clippers, water and dryers. Breeds such as Poodles or Old English Sheepdogs need constant attention to their coats; a professional groomer has the skill and training to ensure dogs leave with unobstructed vision, are comfortable in summer and most importantly he or she will have spotted unwelcome ectoparasites and early signs of skin disease.

'It constantly surprises me that more vets don't encourage their clients to ask for home visits'

Home Visits

Finally, there is always the option of the vet coming to you, at home. This is obviously going to be a more relaxing experience for the pet and it constantly surprises me that more vets don't encourage their clients to ask for home visits. The downside for the vets is that they may have to fight traffic, then perform clinical procedures without the support of a nurse or access to vital equipment. However, that has to be a case-by-case decision. I know of a few pioneering veterinarians who have opted to do all their clinical work in home visits. If minor procedures have to be conducted outside the home, they may have access to a specially converted and high-tech animal ambulance. There are many such inventive alternatives to conventional, surgery-based veterinary practice. What really matters is that there is a good clinical outcome for your dog when he needs veterinary care, and that as far as possible he is not emotionally damaged by the experience.

In the United States, there has been an interesting development of home or domiciliary care for terminally ill pets by trained 'hospice' vets. They specialize in providing old or ill animals with pain relief, management of catheters and generally overseeing their patients' comfort until euthanasia or death takes over. The idea is obviously based upon the concept of palliative care for terminally ill people: a halfway house between aggressive medical intervention and immediate (premature?) euthanasia.

So what we now have is the ultimate expression of the humanization of our man-dog relationship. We treat them as babies when they are puppies, as little people within our family and at the end, before the final goodbye, inflict the same treatment (even the prolonged agony) of an unnaturally delayed death.

9 Caring for the Older Dog

Adapting to a change of pace

Caring for the Older Dog

A dog's later years can be the happiest of times for you both, but he will inevitably become more prone to medical issues. This chapter deals with physical problems such as deafness and arthritis; age-related cognitive impairment; and that painful moment when you may have to decide to end your pet's life.

I have had the great good fortune to live with 12 dogs that reached 10, 12, 14 and PC now a still fit16 years of age, but it was always the last few years that made the greatest emotional impact on me and when I valued their friendship the most. This chapter will dwell upon the particular challenges of caring for your best friend during a period that may also be seen, with the benefit of hindsight, to have been the best of times you spent together.

There are many positive aspects to living with an older dog. They are usually less demanding, more mellow and seemingly more loving

If only old dogs could tell us all the stories about their owners antics!

'Older dogs sleep a lot and they tend not to wreck the house, go walkabout or chase livestock'

than when they were younger. They sleep a lot and they tend not to wreck the house, go walkabout looking for bitches or chase livestock. Unfortunately, in this chapter I am bound to consider the problems more than the pleasures of old age, but in fact many an old dog stays healthy, active and funny until his last breath.

The truth is that dogs are like humans in that they live longer today than in former times, but also in that they sometimes have to pay the price for 'cheating' death which nature had intended to inflict at an earlier age. The obvious common factors which contribute to a longer life in both

humans and dogs are improvements in medical/veterinary care: vaccinations, parasite control, antibiotics and advances in geriatric medicine being the key drivers as far as dogs are concerned.

Genetics also help determine how long a dog lives; little dogs tend to outlive their large-breed cousins and in some cases have double their life expectancy. So it is that Great Danes rarely see their tenth birthday whereas it is common for Jack Russells to reach a score or more years. There are many reasons why this should be so, chief among them being that the heart has to work harder to sustain the metabolic demands of a larger dog.

Medical Issues

Old age is not itself an illness, but an older dog is likely to be more prone to ill health than he was in his younger days. The scourge of old age in dogs is arthritis, which affects joints and inflicts the same chronic pain as we humans experience. But just as arthritis in people can be eased by prescription-only anti-inflammatory drugs, exercise regimes and careful attention to diet, so the same processes and treatments apply to dogs.

But how do we assess discomfort in our dogs? Like most animals, they tend to be stoic when in pain because it is at such times that in natural settings they would be most likely to be killed by a predator or challenged for social dominance by fitter individuals within their group. All the more reason for you to be on the look-out for signs that your best friend is experiencing pain and for assessing his overall quality of life. The starting point for reviewing your dog's welfare is to have the vet conduct a comprehensive annual health assessment, from middle age onwards. He will palpate the major organs, move the limbs, check gums and teeth and commission blood tests to look for early signs of liver disease, diabetes and so on.

It is also well worth developing the discipline of spending a few minutes each day watching your dog and considering if his behaviours and reactions are different from what they used to be.

Sensory Changes: Hearing and Vision

About 50 per cent of dogs over the age of 12 years experience a substantial loss of hearing. The paradox is that some appear to become more sensitive to sounds, but this may be because they are reacting to noises that they used to ignore. Older dogs often seem to be frightened of thunder, fireworks and other such bangs that

Key Indicators of Wellbeing or Declining Health

As your dog ages, watch out for the following:

- **Sleep:** is it fitful, less or more than usual?
- **Responsivity:** does he greet you the way he used to or do you now have to rouse him?
- **Feeding:** does he eat more or less than usual?
- **Movement:** does he walk and run in a co-ordinated fashion, or is he lame and less eager than he used to be when chasing balls and engaging in other doggy games?
- **Vocalizations:** does he whine, yelp or make other noises that you know are associated with distress and pain, especially when he gets up after lying still for a while?
- **Drinking:** is it more or less than usual? Excessive drinking is a likely first indicator of renal disease or of diabetes.

- **Play:** does he still enjoy games with other dogs, especially the rough chase and wrestling that he used to love?

If you see any marked differences in any of these behaviours, as a first step discuss with your vet the short-term prescription of analgesics or anti-inflammatories such as carprofen (marketed as Rimadyl and under various other names). The effect can be remarkable: I have often seen a seemingly depressed, inactive and grumpy dog transformed by being relieved of his chronic pain. However, do not give your dog non-prescription pain-relief medicines that are intended for humans, such as aspirin, ibuprofen or paracetamol.

didn't bother them when they were younger, though total hearing loss may resolve that issue.

I have also had elderly canine patients who were distressed by household sounds such as those from dishwashers, phones or the buzz of insects. But when we test their hearing, we always find a decrease in sensitivity to high-pitched sounds. Some dogs seem to compensate for this loss by having a greater awareness of and possibly a greater sensitivity to low-frequency noises. They then go on to acquire new associations with the world about them, including forming irrational fears of such sounds.

If your dog is going deaf, make an extra effort to stimulate his other senses and involve him in what is going on.

Coping with a Deaf Dog

Practically speaking, you may have to get the attention of a deaf dog by stamping your feet or banging heavy objects together, even using a gong! However, the good news is that dogs are surprisingly quick at learning a substitute for the vocal language you used to share. The standard 'come', 'sit' and ' stay' commands are easily translated into signals using hands, arms and facial expressions. Of course, it is much easier if, in your dog's younger days, you combined vocal and visual signals. Scientific studies indicate that dogs of any age are more responsive to visual signals than they are to the verbal commands which we humans tend to rely upon.

Just as deaf people often remark upon their sense of isolation and of 'being on the outside of events', so it must be for deaf dogs. Make an extra effort to stimulate and communicate with them by other means, such as by sight, touch and even smell. A big practical challenge is finding ways to attract a deaf dog's attention when he is running towards danger and an instant recall response is vital. Fortunately, there is a technological fix available in the form of the radio-controlled

Case Study: Gyp, the Border Collie Who Wouldn't Stop Working

Years ago, we had a working Border Collie on my parents' farm in Devon. Even after his sight deteriorated, old Gyp continued to bring in the cows and move sheep because he knew where every fence, gate and ditch lay. I expect that he also benefited from a compensatory improvement to his senses of smell and hearing. It was lovely to watch him herding sheep, but there was usually one wily ewe who would stand still, away from the main flock, and Gyp would miss her. My father would send him 'back around', but Gyp was plainly frustrated that this one animal did not follow the flock as sheep are meant to do when a Border Collie is about.

The practical implications of this are that blind dogs can experience a good quality of life, although we should not move furniture about unnecessarily and must beware of hazards such as loose cables or an unfenced swimming pool.

vibration collar discussed in Chapter 3. As I said with reference to the problem of deafness in Dalmatians, my experience is that deaf dogs can enjoy a good quality of life and have happy interactions with other dogs and people, even if these are different from the relationships they might have experienced with normal hearing.

Sight Loss

Visual impairment and even total blindness are less common in older dogs than loss of hearing. Fortunately, dogs, like people, are very good at getting the most from what little vision they have. I know of a dog who, by ophthalmological criteria, was considered to be blind but who could in reality detect sufficient light to avoid objects and could follow his owner when she moved.

If you think your dog's sight is failing, ask your veterinarian to monitor it and maybe refer you to a specialist ophthalmologist. Progressive conditions such as cataracts can be treated by surgery in dogs just as they can in people.

Dental Health

There is an epidemic of dental disease in dogs which I attribute mainly to our bad habit of giving them too much industrial pet food (see Chapter 7). A combination of better diet, regular veterinary check-ups and home-based dental hygiene can entirely prevent diseases of the oral cavity. However, the truth is that older dogs tend to suffer from receding gums due to their harbouring chronic infections (periodontitis), which then become a source of recurrent infection to the rest of the body. You can always tell by a dog's breath: is it sweet (though possibly smelling of cow dung!) as opposed to the stench which comes from gas-forming anaerobic bacteria? If the latter, then just imagine the effect on the animal's self-esteem when we humans and maybe other dogs veer away in disgust at their bad breath.

The same pathogenic bacteria jeopardize the health of the rest of an old dog's body, most damagingly when they infect the mitral valves of his heart. Effective care of your dog's teeth is

'Dogs, like people, are very good at getting the most from what little vision they have'

Check your dog's teeth and gums regularly – a healthy mouth makes a major contribution to his welfare.

not a cosmetic luxury; rather it is a life-extending investment in his welfare.

I have long been an enthusiast for the relatively neglected speciality of veterinary dentistry. Inspect your dog's gums regularly, looking for that tell-tale inflamed and bloody line on his gingiva (at the bottom of the teeth). Are any of the teeth broken or infected (they will probably appear blue or black)? Chronic pain from damaged teeth or infected gums can occur in dogs of any age, but is more likely in an elderly animal whose symptoms may be overlooked and wrongly dismissed as the normal frailties of an old dog. I have often seen such dogs undergo a

Myth-Busting: An Old Dog Needn't Make Your Home Smell Unpleasant

In severe cases of urinary incontinence, you can expect to be dealing with a lot of laundry and a regular supply of absorbent towels on plastic sheets may be necessary. I have had clients whose whole household routine was dominated by the care of an elderly and incontinent dog; the smell when I entered the house, plus the state of their carpets, told the tale of their massive devotion, no matter what the cost or the stench. But it doesn't have to be so because incontinent dogs can be trained to accept wearing diapers (nappies).

complete rejuvenation after their dental issues were properly dealt with.

Incontinence and House-Soiling

Old age sometimes brings a breakdown in house-training habits, so that a dog who used to reliably 'last the night' may now begin to urinate and defecate indoors. Maybe he loses bladder control while asleep, if excited during greetings or at other times when aroused and active. These are all classic age-related changes to the neurological control of the bladder and anal sphincters. There may also be deterioration of the peripheral nervous system, with a breakdown in toileting habits being the first symptom to show. German Shepherds tend to be afflicted with a degeneration of the spinal nerves (known as Chronic Degenerative Radiculomyelopathy or CDRM), where sadly they eventually lose control of their hind limbs, bladder and anus even while, during the early stages of the disease, their forelimbs and brain are seemingly

Case Study: Jolene, the Arthritic Collie

A key factor precipitating the breakdown of accustomed toilet habits in dogs may be arthritis and impaired or painful movement, which make them unwilling to get up and 'go' outside. The solution may be as simple as laying a carpet over difficult-to-grip tiled or laminate flooring. Jolene was an elderly Rough (Lassie) Collie who, as is typical of the breed, had excessive hair growing between her toes. She couldn't stand up, let alone walk over the recently laid laminate flooring, so she became less active around the house and had to be helped to the garden. My cure? To install a strip of carpet running the length of the house and to the back door, which Jolene could walk down without fear of slipping. As with many dogs having hairy paws, her stability when walking was also helped by trimming excess fur from between the pads.

As it is with people, so with dogs swimming can be good therapy for a aged limbs and stiff joints.

unaffected. Another cause of incontinence is that the sphincter muscles deteriorate due to a loss in overall tone of the striated (voluntary) muscles and not because of any failure in the nerve supply from the brain.

There are several veterinary approaches to improving toilet function, notably drugs that have an anabolic or strengthening effect upon the musculature, specifically the sphincter muscles. There is every reason to be optimistic about finding a solution to old-age incontinence in dogs, especially if you supplement your vet's advice with commonsensical changes to the way you provide food and water, and continue to give plenty of exercise.

Practical Solutions

If the problem predominantly occurs overnight, shift feeding time to the morning and offer a diet that is easily digestible, contains less fibre and so produces smaller faeces. Except during very hot weather, consider removing the water bowl during the evening so that your dog drinks and urinates earlier in the day.

Signs and Symptoms of Cognitive Impairment: the DISHA Profile

This acronym nicely defines the typical profile of a dog whose brain function has deteriorated, either due to CI or because of damage to the brain following restriction to its arterial blood supply.

- **Disorientation** or getting lost at home or on walks. Maybe the dog goes to the wrong door thinking that it is an exit to the garden, or more subtly he may go to the hinge rather than the opening latch side of the door.
- **Interactions** with people, other dogs and toys all decrease. What responses there are may seem to be of the 'grumpy old man' variety, with the dog not necessarily behaving aggressively but plainly not being as welcoming or as affectionate as he used to be.
- **Sleep/wake cycles** may change so that the dog sleeps a lot during the day but only fitfully at night. This can cause major issues if he pads about the house wanting human company when you just want to sleep.
- **House-training** and other long-established habits may change, some gradually but others quite suddenly. His old quirky ways of greeting you or other habits that set him apart from other dogs may be lost, and with them part of the personality that you have grown to love and to expect.
- **Activity changes** and usually decreases. That means less interest in going for walks, though he may engage in seemingly purposeless pacing, panting and looking as if he is searching for something or someone. Some of these behaviours can be annoying, such as apparently random barking, licking paws, scratching at doors and so on.

Old dogs sometimes forget the toileting habits you instilled in them all those years ago. You may be able to recondition the desired responses by returning to the basics: supervise trips to the garden, then confine to a crate indoors.

Accustom him to going outside to toilet on a frequent and regular basis, perhaps every hour on the hour signalled by an alarm such as from an oven timer. Going to the garden then becomes a Pavlovian conditioned response whose payoff is a treat or titbit. Yes, old dogs as well as young can be trained to toilet on command by using a reward-based, classical conditioning strategy.

It may be that urinary or faecal incontinence is a sign of general cognitive impairment and memory loss. The dog has simply forgotten that the place to toilet is outside. In such a case, you may have to return to the fundamental training principles you employed in the puppy era. Dust off that crate or borrow one from a friend who has just graduated to allowing his puppy the freedom of the house, and use it as a positive training aid. Again, apply Pavlovian conditioning

Do Sex Hormones Prevent Cognitive Impairment?

Human studies have consistently shown that the female hormone oestrogen and its male counterpart testosterone help protect against AD. Benjamin Hart in California has published a study monitoring the effects of castration in dogs upon the development of age-related cognitive impairment, and his findings are in line with the human literature. There does seem to be a genuine neuro-protective role for both testosterone and oestrogen at the cellular level, which at least slows down the development of Alzheimer's in people and of cognitive impairment in dogs.

This finding could be taken as controversial justification for not spaying bitches or castrating dogs. However, for bitches, this has to be balanced against the well-documented benefits which spaying confers upon health and life expectancy; for instance it dramatically reduces the incidence of mammary tumours. Castrated dogs are less likely to have life-threatening behavioural problems.

principles: take him from the crate to the garden on the signal of a regular bell, and be on hand to reward him for urinating or defecating.

Finally, dogs are more likely to acquire bladder infections as they grow older because, like elderly people, they have less robust immune systems

How You Can Help

All five of the key signs of CI (see box) can occur in dogs of any age and for reasons unconnected with deterioration in brain function. However, taken in combination, when two or more signs occur and are not associated with other physical

'Just as many elderly people remain as bright as buttons, so it is that some lucky old dogs stay sharp to the end'

than youngsters. Monitor your dog's urine for tell-tale signs of blood (catch a few drops on clean white tissue). Antibiotic therapy may be the answer, so consult your vet.

Old Age Cognitive Impairment or Canine Dementia

As with people, we can expect our dogs to have some degree of memory loss and impaired ability to learn new tasks as they grow old. However, there are enormous individual differences and, just as many elderly people remain as bright as buttons, so it is that some lucky old dogs stay sharp to the end.

Unfortunately, the canine equivalent of Alzheimer's Disease (AD) and its associated dementia can also affect many elderly dogs. It is strictly age-related, with the result that large breeds with their shorter life spans are less likely to show indications of Old Age Cognitive Impairment (CI) than longer-lived small or medium-sized dogs.

The age of onset and the speed of development of CI is just as variable in dogs as AD is in people. A study, by Professor Benjamin Hart and colleagues at the University of Davis, California, of dogs aged 15–16 years found that 65 per cent showed some sign of mental impairment and half of those were severely impaired. The key indicators of CI are shown in the box on page 171.

illnesses (such as heart or respiratory disease), then the dog is in all likelihood suffering from CI. So what can be done to slow down the process and give an affected dog the best quality of life for as long as possible?

The most important single thing you can do to keep your dog young is to act young. Take him for walks, play complicated hide-and-seek games in the woods and challenge him with those interactive board games, invented by Nina Ottosson, that are described in Chapter 4. Maybe this is a time to consider bringing in a younger and more stimulating canine companion: stories of how old dogs are rejuvenated by a pestering puppy or a newly adopted adult are legion.

Elderly dogs who have seemed to be on their last legs often have a new lease of life when you introduce a playful new puppy to the family.

Post-mortem examination of the brains from elderly dogs with advanced cognitive impairment have shown that the frontal cortex (associated with memory and learning) and the hippocampus (also associated with cognitive behaviour) tend to accumulate deposits similar to the plaques that characterize the brains of humans suffering from AD. Research suggests that accumulation of these plaques can be reduced by dietary supplements and specifically by antioxidants and drugs that improve or affect mitochondrial function. However, just as with elderly people, the best way for a dog to stay fit is by exercise and taking an appropriate, healthy diet, as described in Chapter 7.

Drug Therapies

There are two drug therapies for CI showing promising results in trials, backed up by the experience of vets in practice. Propentofylline, marketed as Vivitonin, has been licensed in a number of countries for many years and is claimed by the manufacturers to increase oxygen supply to the brain by improving blood flow.

gustatory senses (which are often surprisingly resilient and do not generally deteriorate) with interesting smells and tastes. As in many other respects, the needs of an old dog are remarkably like the needs of elderly people.

Decision Time: When to Say Goodbye

Dogs are privileged because we can prevent them from suffering in old age by deciding to end their lives. If possible, share this responsibility with others, especially your vet. He or she is best placed to assess the dog's quality of life and, if yours is suffering and unlikely to return to good health, guide you towards euthanasia.

However, the criteria which individual vets apply to this issue vary enormously and it can be very unkind if you are made to feel you are being pushed towards expensive long-term care option for a pet suffering from, say, terminal cancer. I have no doubt that some dogs are kept alive for too long by overly sophisticated life-support systems, which deny them dignity and prolong emotional conflicts in the owner. Somewhere

'Dogs are privileged because we can prevent them from suffering in old age by deciding to end their lives'

More controversial is selegiline, which seems to slow down the rate of impairment in cognitive function in some dogs. Marketed in the UK as Selgian and in North America as Anipryl, it has been licensed only relatively recently and its efficacy for improving the longevity and welfare of elderly dogs remains uncertain.

The one therapy that definitely helps to conserve mental function in old dogs is a combination of stimulation, activity and interest. Don't leave your faithful old friend to sleep his life away; rather involve him in interesting activities and stimulate his olfactory and

there is a middle ground between overly quick euthanasia of a still happy animal and extending the life of a dog facing shutdown of key organ systems, inability to walk and, importantly, loss of dignity because he is no longer able to control vital toileting functions.

There are differences of opinion about whether the act of euthanasia should be dealt with at the veterinary clinic or at home. As a matter of convenience to the vet it may be accomplished more easily at his clinic. However, my experience tells me that it is better for the dog if it is done at home, where he is calm and

Home is the best place for children to say goodbye to a beloved pet once you have taken the tough decision to end his days.

where other family members and even other pets can, to some small extent, be involved. Home is a better place for you to say a kind goodbye. It is the time to indulge your old friend with his favourite garlic sausage or other delicacy, and to hold him in your arms as he slips away. Tears are allowed! From an animal's point of view, the experience will be literally falling into a deep slumber, just as we experience when we are anaesthetized in hospital or at the dentist. There need be no suffering in this process of dying from an anaesthetic overdose.

I am often asked if other dog(s) or even cats of the household should be allowed contact with the deceased pet. I have had the privilege of watching these final interactions between animals that have lived together for many years, and I do believe that it helps to reduce the grieving process for them as it does for us. Animals clearly recognize when another is dead, as opposed to having just 'gone missing'.

Another question is what to do with the body? If you live in the city there may be no alternative except to cremate, but burial in the garden or even in a designated pet cemetery provides a physical location where you can go to mourn and reconnect with the past that you shared. The grieving process is bound to be painful, but for some it can be impossible to deal with alone. In cases of prolonged pathological grieving for a lost pet, help can be sought from professional counsellors. In the United Kingdom, the charity Society of Companion Animal Studies (SCAS) provides just such a service. Its helplines are manned by trained individuals who understand what you are feeling because they too have loved and lost a special animal companion.

10 A Better Place for Dogs

What next for dog culture?

A Better Place for Dogs

The special place of dogs in our lives. A look at good and bad treatment, past and present. The future for dogs as companion animals in our over-populated and over-urbanized world. Extreme dogs, both large and small. The increasing popularity of dogs in developing countries – where is it leading?

Dogs have a very special relationship with people because they are the only species that seemingly volunteer to join us without the need for cages or chains of captivity. Contrast that with the way other animals are kept as pets: reptiles, rodents and birds have to be imprisoned behind glass or wire in a way that most of us would deem unacceptable if it were applied to dogs. Dogs choose to stay around people as our friends, guardians and entertainers, becoming part of the human family, not merely a hobby or an adjunct to it. In their different way, cats retain their wild and independent disposition by choosing human

Dogs are continuing to fulfill the role of companions in our increasingly atomized modern society.

'Dogs choose to stay around people as our friends, guardians and entertainers'

company and habitation, without the need for chains or bars. By doing so of their own free will, both species flatter us.

However, dogs continue to be exposed to sinister uses and abuses: in laboratory research, for organized fighting (still legal in many countries and a lucrative 'black market' business in the West) and as food. Archaeological evidence reveals that the practice of eating dogs was widespread throughout history and pre-history in Europe, Asia and the Americas. Today it continues mainly in Asia, where it is estimated that 13–16 million dogs are consumed

every year, and not just by the poor and hungry. There are many people who believe that dog meat has health-promoting properties, even in technologically advanced countries such as South Korea, where dogs are also kept as pets and are, for the most part, treated kindly.

In poor and non-industrialized societies, the contradiction between having dogs both as companions and as a source of meat seems to be resolved by their value as a buffer food resource, to be eaten when crops fail and hunger stalks. Our European taboo against eating dog may itself be of only recent origin, a luxury that has come about because, relatively speaking, food has become a cheap commodity for the masses. However, in extreme circumstances, even we might abandon our principled distaste for eating dog: witness the Norwegian explorer Amundsen, who raced his dogs to the South Pole while his party ate them one by one as the need arose. Captain Scott, the unlucky Englishman, had his men haul sledges to the South Pole themselves, and wouldn't contemplate eating dog. Yet we know that Amundsen made it to the Pole and back and that all of Scott's party perished. So who was right?

I would like to think that we are living in a golden age of understanding and appreciation of dogs. Unfortunately, the sad reality is that in post-industrial Britain, North America and indeed all the world's major urban societies, dogs and dog-keeping are too often threatened by the imposition of petty rules and restrictions, and sometimes by blatantly anti-dog legislation. Let's take the British example of how dogs are treated now, compared to in the past.

Is Britain Really a Dog-loving Nation?

Every three or four months, the tabloid newspapers feature a ghastly dog attack in which the 'victim' suffers terrible injuries and lurid photographs draw attention to the dangerous side of canine behaviour. My heart sinks when such stories appear, because I know that my phone will soon be ringing with calls from the BBC, Sky and other major broadcasters wanting me to explain why such things happen and, even better, give a one-minute recipe for avoiding such disasters in future.

I have been living with these stories throughout my professional life and the British media know very well that, rather than give a 'quick fix', I will always look to the complex underlying causes of such terrible events as when, for instance, a child is mauled by the family's pet dog. As I discussed in Chapter 2, the Breed Specific Legislation or BSL that is in place in many countries is no solution. For me this has led to a 20-year battle with an insane court system that criminalizes owners for having dogs

Even today, working dogs have a role to play. In some snowy wastelands of the Arctic Circle, dog sled is still the most practical way to travel.

Training never stops and should involve all of the family who can all be trained to use the clicker and other reward based training methods.

that look a certain way, irrespective of how they behave. Protests in the United States, Europe, Australia and elsewhere have lobbied to bring BSL to an end with the clarion call of 'punish the deed, not the breed', but they have been largely ignored by their respective governments.

Thirty years' work to resolve canine behavioural problems has made me pessimistic about the future of dogs in society. And why? Primarily because so many of the problems that I and other professionals see arise because of failures in training, specifically by trainers who use an unbalanced, over-indulgent, 'reward-based' philosophy. The unfortunate consequence has been that dogs take control of their people because no one has established the boundaries within which the dogs must operate. In a word, discipline! Dogs are quintessentially social animals that interact with one another and with people according to definite rules of dominance, subordinance and deference. I do not side with the dog trainers who overuse expressions like 'top dog' and 'be the leader', while interpreting almost every facet of dog behaviour in terms of social dominance and a failure of owners to be that top dog.

(not a comparison that stands up to scientific scrutiny!), but just as children are spoilt by random overindulgence, so are dogs if they are not penalized for unacceptable behaviours. What is or is not acceptable is a matter of personal choice and of circumstances, so that, for instance, a barking dog may be regarded as a problem in a high-rise apartment block, but be seen as a bonus on an isolated farm where it deters robbers.

'Dogs are quintessentially social animals that interact according to definite rules of dominance and deference'

However, at the other extreme, there are those who pretend that social hierarchies in dogs don't exist – a claim that has about the same calibre of intellectual rigour as denying that the earth is round or that Hitler initiated the holocaust. These arguments are daft and dangerous in roughly equal measure, because they create too many undisciplined and seemingly uncontrollable dogs. The mental development or intelligence of adult dogs is often likened to that of a two-, three-, four- or five-year-old child

The Mugford method is, as you will now appreciate, about balance, with owners like you acquiring the techniques needed to create unambiguous traffic lights that indicate to dogs what they may or may not do. There is a penalty if a dog acts on the equivalent of a red light, a payoff for behaviours signalled by green. The only skills you require are to determine what does or does not motivate your dog and to deliver payoffs and penalties in a fair and timely fashion. What could be simpler?

Dogs are the most
exuberant honest
of entertainers.

Dogs and People

About half of the planet earth's seven billion
people live in cities, cut off from the everyday
natural experiences that come from watching
animals on farms, in forests or in the oceans.
More influenced by Disney than by Darwin, they
may then fantasize about animal emotions and
turn animals into little humanized characters,
to be either fawned over or feared. Skilful use
of muscles and movement to control a flighty
animal such as a horse is substituted by the
offering up of a carrot or sugar lump. Carrots
and sugar lumps don't always work on horses
and nor do they on dogs.

Ancestral fear of predators such as lions,
tigers or, closer to the subject, wolves has been
substituted by fear of dogs, spiders and bacteria.
It is no longer a very brave world, but one in
which the poor dog has somehow to make do.
No wonder that animal psychologists such as
myself are in demand.

A Dog's Role in the Modern Age

In order to consider this question, we need to
realize that dogs are an integral part of nature in
an otherwise mostly man-made world. As such,
they enable us to look into the natural world
and to better understand how it works. Consider
life with your dog as an alternative to reading

Charles Darwin or his modern equivalent,
Richard Dawkins.

This age of the Internet has changed the
pace and quality of human social behaviour:
local connections to neighbours still count, but
social media such as Facebook put thousands or
millions in touch who share common interests,
including an interest in dogs. There are countless
forums for dog lovers (and haters!) and websites
galore with advice on this and that to do
with dogs, their care, training and behaviour.
Unfortunately, much of the information is
wrong, contradictory and unhelpful, particularly
if it is written for dogs in general rather than
for the experiences affecting an individual dog/
human interaction. For those of us who like to
celebrate the individuality of our relationship
with dogs, the broad-brush approach of dos and
don'ts is irrelevant.

The enduring human needs for love,
recognition and fun are not always to be satisfied
by an online existence. So dogs are unlikely
to become redundant or unfashionable at any
time in the foreseeable future. Their gift of
companionship will always be necessary to make
people's lives better, especially for the young
and the elderly, who for different reasons can
find themselves detached from mainstream
society and lonely. But then again, dogs are

good for us no matter what our age or financial circumstances.

Little and Large

There are conflicting trends in dog ownership that seem to appeal to different sides of human nature: on the one hand, gigantic dogs with a macho and even dangerous image; at the other extreme, miniature 'pocket' or handbag specimens. The reality is that, generally speaking, both the little and the large satisfy similar human needs, despite the incongruous contrast between, say, a Great Dane and a Chihuahua.

The fashion for miniature dogs has been encouraged by photo-shoots with Paris Hilton and other celebs featuring Yorkshire Terriers, Maltese and the like that can weigh less than 1kg, some even half that (ie. a pound). Are these tiny creatures still dogs? Yes, because despite the extreme physical changes, their instincts and behavioural needs remain wholly canine.

Many of the tiny dogs that come to us for treatment are highly intolerant of others: they were not socialized as puppies because their owners were worried that they might be hurt – or worse – by larger dogs. I understand their concern, but that is no reason for neglecting a puppy's training or learning of social skills. This over-protectiveness on the part of the owners is fuelling a rise in numbers of emotionally disturbed miniature dogs that are aggressive to both people and others dogs. Threats by small dogs often incite a reciprocal attack from larger ones, which will easily inflict injury and 'be blamed' for the incident. Meanwhile, rehoming agencies are everywhere faced with large numbers of unwanted giants and pygmies: they can be difficult to place into suitable homes.

Case Study: Rich or Poor, Dogs Work the Same Magic

I have a client, Kevin, who is homeless and lives rough on the streets or in the derelict buildings of prosperous Windsor. I have another client in the same town who lives in the castle. Both love their dogs: Kevin his black Labrador, Buster, and the Queen her corgis. The extraordinary contrast of circumstances between the two hit me when I examined Buster in the public grounds below the castle ramparts, as a preliminary to giving evidence on Kevin's behalf in a court case. Buster has survived three tough winters keeping Kevin warm and safe. Unfortunately, that included barking aggressively and even lunging at well-intentioned police officers concerned for Kevin's welfare as he slept in doorways.

During my first examination of Buster, I saw that he never took his eyes off Kevin, but rather followed him everywhere and responded to the most complex conversational instructions such as, 'Now you stay here, I'll be back in ten minutes.' They played hide and seek, fetch and all the silly things that we dog people do, except that for Kevin and Buster it was more a matter of life and death, keeping Kevin warm, fit, sane and sober in a harsh world.

After another minor incident, Buster was eventually taken from Kevin and locked up in police kennels pending a hearing that could have sentenced him to death. Happily, the court showed compassion and Buster was ordered into our care: he now lives in our home in unaccustomed doggy luxury, with warmth, the certainty of regular meals and companionship from the Mugford family of dogs. But will Kevin survive his separation from Buster?

Old English Sheepdogs suddenly became popular during the 1960s in the UK because of a TV advert for paint. Now they are a rarity.

Toy breeds have become the latest must-have accessory courtesy of Hollywood lifestyle.

Fashions change and with them the popularity of this or that breed of dog. After World War II Dobermans (the unkindly and undeservedly nicknamed 'Devil Dogs') were the in thing. Then it was fluffy to the point of nearly blind Old English Sheepdogs, followed by wrinkled Shar Peis (a dermatological disaster), Pit Bulls, other so-called status dogs and now the teeny weenies. *Plus ça change*, but what next?

where dogs can be segregated for off-leash play and to toilet. Human nature being what it is, and there being no obvious payoff for picking up canine excrement, it is right that penalties should be imposed on those who do not. Poop-scoop laws have worked wonders in cleaning up cities around the world, thereby neutralizing one of the all-too-frequently recurring arguments from those who dislike dogs.

'We are fortunate that Victorian town planners took the view that cities needed green spaces. They were right!'

Dogs in the City

Cities can never be an ideal place for a dog to live, but for many that is the way it has to be. I said in Chapter 8 that apartment living need not be a bad option for dogs, so long as owners make the investment in time to take them for walks in the park, forest or wilderness. In the UK, we are fortunate that Victorian town planners took the view that cities needed green spaces for working people to enjoy on their rest days. They were right! But city parks must not be allowed to degenerate into mere dog latrines, so sensible city authorities divide them up and provide spaces

City parks are boring if they are nothing more than open, featureless and flat spaces. Dogs like to explore untamed semi-wilderness where there are thickets and dense undergrowth, places that also provide good habitats for birds and other wildlife. In Germany, it is common to find gymnastic equipment in parks and forest trails provided free for the use of walkers, runners and, of course, dog owners. It would be only a small positive step to cater for the needs of dogs too, by supplying fixed sets of agility equipment such as rings for them to jump, poles to weave in and out of and seesaws to climb. Access to such facilities

Playing with our dogs brings tangible health benefits to us both.

country you care to mention seems to be on the up. The company of dogs has become a near-universal want, because dogs satisfy a number of important emotional needs in people, such as giving and receiving affection, which in turn massively enhances our self-esteem.

There is compelling scientific evidence that dogs bring tangible psychological and medical benefits to their people. They help us to live longer, if only because we are less stressed and take more exercise. Studies show that dog owners are physically healthier, more sociable, psychologically better adjusted and can boast more human friendships than non-dog owners or declared dog haters. These benefits particularly affect certain social groups, namely those with disabilities, those with a sedentary lifestyle who benefit from increased exercise, and young couples in the process of home formation. For them, a house is not a home unless it is shared with another living thing and many acquire a dog in anticipation of starting their own human family.

The future for dogs and dog ownership should be better now than it has ever been because

might encourage both dogs and people to exercise and even stir up their competitive sides.

An American company, Barkpark, from Red Bud, Illinois, is ahead of the game: with the corporate mission to 'make your dog park a community destination', it manufactures an

'The future for dogs and dog ownership should be better now than it has ever been'

innovative range of robust fittings that dogs can seesaw, jump and explore. But the number one game all dogs enjoy: throwing a ball to retrieve … or to grab, run and be chased.

The Future

In most of the world, including China, India, Brazil and others of the fast-developing countries, living with dogs is increasingly popular. Economic recessions come and go, but the number of dogs in North America, Europe, Japan, Korea and almost every other

of multiple advances in canine genetics and veterinary care, and the more intelligent design of urban landscapes that protects dogs, children and the rest of us from the ever-present danger of traffic. City planners should try to meet this challenge by striking a more dog-friendly balance between our hunger for personal mobility (ie. the car) and provision of safe open spaces.

Dogs and children are the key movers that drive this process in both town and country. Just as important, governments need to ensure that dog owners have legal rights of access to wilderness, forest and other such open spaces, instead of having to negotiate fences and face unreasonable threats from hunting interests or selfish property owners. Many dogs are legally shot in German forests owned by hunting syndicates, or in Spain during their chaotic open shooting season. On the other hand, we

favourable treatment by landlords, in restaurants and other places from which dogs are so often excluded. The good thing about dogs is that they don't accumulate gadgets, drive cars or generally destroy the planet. Our two species have evolved a wonderfully symbiotic relationship, though people always have to exert ultimate control,

'The good thing about dogs is that they don't accumulate gadgets, drive cars or generally destroy the planet'

dog owners have to respect wildlife (except for squirrels!) and farm livestock, because to do so is a matter of animal welfare, economics and common sense.

Setting aside complaints about the noise of dogs barking and fouling, keeping dogs should be viewed as a positive lifestyle choice, and we do pay taxes for the privilege of having dogs! In return, we can reasonably expect more

set the rules and when necessary invoke a just regime of payoffs and penalties for the dogs we love. I hope that this book will help you to achieve that goal with your dog.

Enjoying the affection and fun of dogs has been one of the most rewarding experiences of my life. May it be the same for you.

Index

Acknowledgements

Many thousands of dog owners have contributed to this book by sharing their experiences and problems with me over three decades of my work as an applied animal psychologist. I thank them all and hope they got some benefit from the experience. Whilst absent from our Behaviour Centre and writing this book, the good work continued under the guidance of Karen Hill, a friend and colleague of many years.

Special thanks go to my wife Marissa for her patience and persistent encouragement, even when I was distracted by having too much fun on the farm or whilst travelling around the world.

Credit for the design of this book goes to the wonderful team at Octopus Publishing Group, the project having been initiated by Trevor Davies, then critically edited by Joanne Wilson and Caroline Taggart. Thanks to them and to my friend and motivator Faith Evans for making it all happen.

I am very grateful to the dogs and people who gave up their time to appear in this book, with special thanks to trainers Wendy King, Hannah Smith and Fiona Whelan. Stars of the photoshoots are Bounce, Humphrey, P.C., Lily, Bubba, Buttons, Charli, Star, Shyla, Sancho, Noux and Orejas and it is to them and their canine companions that I dedicate the book in the optimistic hope that things will keep getting better for them, wherever in the world they may be.

Commissioned Photography copyright Adrian Pope/Octopus Publishing Group

Other photography: age footstock/ArenaCreative 162 left; FLPA/Angela Hampton 159; H. Schmidt-Roeger 162 right. Alamy/Aurora Photos/ Karl Schatz 160; blickwinkel/ Schmidt-Roeger 17 below right; Jack Cox – Images of Nature 175; Daniel Dempster Photography 17 below centre; O. Digoit 4 above; Farlap 17 below left, 28 above left; John Henshall 170; Wayne Hutchinson 28 below right; imagebroker/Harald Theissen 178; Juniors Bildarchiv GmbH 15 below right, 102; Christina Kennedy 5; Garry Lakin 28 below left; Ovia Images/O.Digoit 21; PhotoAlto/es/Eric Planchard 42 above left; RIA Novosti 69; TNT Magazine 34; Petra Wegner 137; wonderlandstock 141. Ardea/Jean Paul Ferrero 135. Coolzonedog.com, manufactured by HTFx Inc., Melbourne, Florida 157. Company of animals 4, 5 Corbis/Birgid Allig 32; dpa/Jan Woitas 118 below; Tim Graham 179; National Geographic Society 15 below left; Swim Ink 2, LLC 15 above left. Dr. Roger Mugford 37, 100, 101, 108 right, 171. Getty Images/Brian Asmussen 84; Barcroft Media via Getty Images 31; De Agostini 10; Jamie Grill 183; GK Hart/Vikki Hart 153; Tim Ridley 79 right; Siri Stafford 28 centre left; your personal camera obscura 154. Medical Detection Dogs 20. Octopus Publishing Group 134 below, 138, 143; Rosie Hyde 185; Geoff Langan 57, 67, 126, 158, 161, 166, 168, 169, 172, 173, 184; Ray Moller 15 centre left, 15 above right; Angus Murray 43 below right; Russell Sadur 97, 127 left, 127 right, 130, 134 above, 136, 144, 145, 156, 180. Press Association Images/ Sue Ogrocki/AP 14 left. RSPCA Photolibrary147; Andrew Forsyth 133. Science Photo Library/Thierry Berrod, Mona Lisa Production 11 left; Gustoimages 105; D. Roberts 11 right. Shutterstock/leungchopan 51; Okeanas 150; Scorpp 163. SuperStock/Juniors 63. The Bridgeman Art Library/Photo © Bonhams, London, UK 15 centre right. The Company of Animals Ltd. 146. Thinkstock/Michael Blann 16; Digital Vision 176; Hemera 42 below right, 42 above right; iStockphoto 28 centre right, 28 above right, 42 below left, 59, 183 left. www.anxietywrap.com 115 left.

Commissioning Editor Trevor Davies
Editor Jo Wilson
Copy-Editor Caroline Taggart
Deputy Art Director Yasia Williams-Leedham
Designer Isabel de Cordova
Art Director, Photoshoot Alison Fenton
Photographer Adrian Pope
Assistant Production Manager Lucy Carter
Production Controller Alexandra Bell
Picture Researcher Jennifer Veall
Proofreader Julia Rolf
Indexer Diana LeCore